All My Patients Kick and Bite

ALSO BY JEFF WELLS

All My Patients Have Tales

The Veterinarian's Handbook for Horse Husbands

All My Patients Kick and Bite

More Favorite Stories from a Vet's Practice

Jeff Wells, D.V.M.

Illustrations by June Camerer

St. Martin's Press ❧ New York

ALL MY PATIENTS KICK AND BITE. Copyright © 2011 by Jeff Wells. All rights reserved. Printed in the United States of America. For information, address St. Martin's Press, 175 Fifth Avenue, New York, N.Y. 10010.

www.stmartins.com

Illustrations by June Camerer

Library of Congress Cataloging-in-Publication Data

Wells, Jeff, D.V.M.
    All my patients kick and bite : more favorite stories from a vet's practice / Jeff Wells.—1st ed.
        p. cm.
    ISBN 978-0-312-66812-9
    1. Wells, Jeff, D.V.M.—Anecdotes.   2. Veterinarians—Anecdotes.
3. Veterinary medicine—Practice—Colorado—Anecdotes.
4. Veterinarians—Colorado—Biography—Anecdotes.   I. Title.
    SF745.W465 2011
    636.089092—dc23
    [B]

                                                                2011024756

First Edition: October 2011

10 9 8 7 6 5 4 3 2 1

I dedicate this book to my clients,
who have trusted me to care for their pets over the years.

Contents

Acknowledgments

I want to thank my agent, Jacques de Spoelberch, for his continual guidance, and my editor, Daniela Rapp, for her enduring patience.

I also want to thank Jenny Hancey, Mary Anne Mier, Julia Nichols, and Jenny Ramsey for all their help.

Last, I want to thank my wife, Marion, and daughter, Jin, for allowing me to be distracted temporarily while I wrote this book.

All My Patients Kick and Bite

Animal Control

It was almost five o'clock and Miss Sloan had not shown up at the clinic yet. She was scheduled to bring in her dog Toby, a two-year-old bloodhound–Weimaraner cross, by four o'clock to be treated for an ear infection. I had met Miss Sloan only once before, when she brought in a vomiting puppy after hours. She was a single, rather eccentric woman who lived in a fairly remote area with twelve unneutered dogs. She never brought them in for vaccinations or routine procedures. The only time we saw them was when there was a major problem. The dogs, not unlike their owner, were not overly socialized, to say the least. They so rarely saw people that it made them extremely skittish when they were exposed to strangers.

"I tried to call her, but no one answered. She must be on her way," Lorraine, our frequently blunt middle-aged receptionist, said to Christie and me as she walked out the door for the evening. "Be sure to lock up when you are done."

Christie, my faithful, yet sometimes reluctant, young veterinary assistant, and I had already had a long day. We were just about ready to leave ourselves, when an old monster sedan pulled into the driveway, coughing smoke from at least three sides of its undercarriage. The metal dragon coasted into a parking space and backfired as the engine shut down. Out of the driver's side appeared a seventy-year-old woman with unkempt gray hair, an antique ski jacket, and tan leather work boots. We could not help but notice a large dog bouncing around in the backseat while Miss Sloan fumbled with a leash. Christie went out to give her a hand while I got some sedative pulled up and ear cleansers set out so we could speed up the process. Just then, I heard some yelling coming from the parking lot.

Toby had freaked out, biting Miss Sloan on the right hand when she tried to get the leash on him. By the time I made it to the front door, he had leaped from the car and was running full speed across the highway into the subdivision on the other side. His long ears were flapping and his skinny tail was wagging good-bye to us. Miss Sloan held her lacerated right hand with her left as the blood seeped between the fingers of her good hand.

"Please don't hurt him," she cried. "He's just not used to people or being confined."

We certainly had no intention of hurting her pet, but we absolutely had to get him back. When an unvaccinated animal bites a person, the possibility of rabies becomes a huge issue. Legally, the animal has to be quarantined for two weeks, or a tissue sample from the animal has to be sent to a rabies-testing laboratory. Let's just say that the tissues required cannot be taken from a live animal. If the suspect animal cannot be found, the bite victim must start a rather painful series of injection to counteract the rabies virus. Once a victim shows symptoms of rabies, it is usually too late to treat them successfully. We were going to have to find Toby.

"Miss Sloan, you will have to see a doctor about those wounds," I told her as I examined her punctured hand.

She started to object, but Christie backed me up. "You need to drive directly to the medical office. You don't want to get an infection. Do let them know that Toby wasn't vaccinated." Miss Sloan agreed, wrapped her hand in some gauze, and headed down the road.

Now we had to deal with Toby. "Christie, call Animal Control and tell them what's going on," I told her. "We will have to file a report; then they can try to find Toby."

After Christie made the call, I sent her home and then waited for an officer to come by. About ten minutes later, a Ford Bronco with ANIMAL CONTROL printed in huge letters on the side roared up the driveway and a short, plump man in a uniform jumped out. I had worked with Johnny several times before on animal-abuse cases. He was a really nice guy and took his job very seriously.

"Hey, Doc! Sounds like we've got a little adventure on our hands!" he announced exuberantly. Johnny was about twenty-six years old and still completely enamored of his career choice. "We just got a new tranquilizer gun in, and I think today is the day to try it out," he added. You would have thought we were going after an escaped rhino, not a scared canine. This was going to be interesting.

Officer Johnny had me fill out a little paperwork on the bite incident and Toby's lack of vaccination history. "Well, saddle up," he instructed me. "Let's go find him."

I was planning on searching for Toby, but not in the Animal Control vehicle. I could see, however, that it was going to be impossible to turn Johnny down, so I reluctantly crawled into the passenger side, kicking enough empty soda bottles out of the way to find a place for my feet. Johnny yanked the gearshift into drive. The rear tires dug into the gravel driveway, and we were off. I don't know which smelled worse, the burning rubber or the overstuffed ashtray.

I heard Johnny say under his breath, "This is going to be so much fun." It was obvious that he had watched too many cop shows and had forgotten that we were chasing a confused canine, not a hard-ened criminal.

We bounced down the driveway, across the highway, and into the unsuspecting subdivision. Johnny tore through the streets, passing cedar-sided houses and spinning out in the cul-de-sacs to change direction and check another street.

"He has to be around here somewhere. He couldn't have gotten too far!" Johnny all but squealed with the glee of a schoolboy.

Luckily, it was dinnertime and all the children and their parents were inside eating. This whole episode was quickly becoming the high-light of Johnny's week, and he was having way too much fun. After about the fifth street, and right at the peak of my car sickness, Johnny spotted Toby running behind a house and brought the Bronco to a sliding stop just in time to keep me from vomiting.

"Let's get the tranq gun loaded while he is hiding. We'll be ready for him when he comes out." I wanted to reply, You've got to be kid-ding me, but I didn't, as he seemed determined that this was the best way to capture the freaked-out canine.

Since I couldn't come up with a better, less stressful way to con-vince Toby to go back to the clinic with us, I let Johnny proceed with his over-the-top plan. He fumbled to fill the tiny dart with a couple milliliters of sedative that we supplied to the Animal Control officers for just such an occasion. It appeared that this may have been the first time that this "big-game hunter" had actually darted an animal. Once the dart was loaded, he had to decide exactly how it fit into the gun. He held the apparatus up so that I could see, as well.

"What do you think, Doc?" he asked with a tinge of embarrass-ment in his voice. It was a new type of tranquilizer dart, so I was no help, and it was nothing like the large darts that I had used on buf-falo in the past.

"You are on your own on this one," I explained. "I have no idea." Subconsciously, I think, I just really didn't want any part in this debacle. I could not believe we were going to dart the poor thing, yet it was better than Toby getting hit by a car while on his escapade.

"Well, I guess I will just have to go for it. I hope that I can hit him!" Johnny said with a hint of disgust in his voice.

He did not seem to be pleased with my lack of expertise on the subject at hand. He mumbled, "I sure hope that this is right," then placed the dart in the tranquilizer pistol and held it in the open window of the Bronco's driver-side door, waiting for Toby to reappear from behind the house. Time seemed to slow to a standstill.

We sat silently in the cab of the vehicle, waiting for Toby to show himself again. At first, I told myself that it wouldn't be long now, but then I began to wonder if he would ever come out. What could he possibly be doing back there? My mind began to wander. I imagined he had met other dogs back there and they were having a party, laughing about Johnny and me waiting in the truck. I pulled myself back from the edge and began counting the seconds between Johnny's deep breaths. Johnny finally began to fidget. Up until now, he had held his ground quite well, but he was beginning to break.

"Where in heck is that dog?" he muttered. I almost brought up my theory of the dog party going on behind the house, but then thought better of it. Johnny might not see the humor in my imagination.

Of course, what seemed like an hour was in reality probably only ten minutes. The sun had just dropped behind the pine trees when I made out the tip of a nose and a dark eye peering around the corner of the house. It always amazes me how animals instinctively know exactly what you are up to. Johnny tightened the grip on his pistol while Toby made his way from behind the house into the shadows of the swing set a few feet away. From there, he could easily have made the twenty feet between the swing set and the next house. In a matter of minutes, darkness would be his teammate and we would be out of luck for the night. But Toby made a break for it a little too early, and I cringed when the trigger on Johnny's tranquilizer gun clicked. I expected the next sound to be yelping as the dart punctured Toby's skin. Instead, Toby stopped short, looking a little confused by the dart now lodged firmly in the metal support post of the swing set behind him. We had successfully sedated a child's toy.

If dogs can laugh, Toby laughed at us. He was smiling from ear to ear, tongue fully extended. Even his eyes gleamed as he stared us down in defiance. Now the chase had become a game for him, and he was winning. Toby lifted his leg and urinated on the swing set as if it were his trophy. He wagged his tail, turned, and pranced off into the dark.

"Now what do we do?" asked a less enthusiastic Johnny.

"We retrieve the dart from the swing set and call it a night," I replied. "The next thing we hit might not be as innocuous."

This comment seemed to get the point across to Johnny, and he sank down into the seat while he drove me back to the clinic after prying the dart from its metal victim. I got out of the truck and said good night to Johnny.

The clinic was dark except for the glow from the small yellowish lightbulb above the door. The stars were bright, not a cloud in the sky and not a sign of Toby. The Colorado night air made me shiver a little. It was either time to go home or to come up with a new plan. The clock behind the reception desk read 8:00 P.M. as I unlocked the door to the clinic. I couldn't stand to think that Toby might be running around out there in the night with mountain lions, bears, and every dog's worst enemy—cars—on the prowl. I sat at my desk and leaned back in the chair, desperately trying to think of a way to retrieve the elusive dog, but all the awful ways that Toby could meet his demise kept running through my head, blocking my ability to come up with a solution. I was sure that Johnny was home by now, probably in front of the television, a beer in hand, a feeling that the ball was back in my court. He'd be free of any guilt, since he had literally given Toby his best shot.

I walked to the front door of the clinic and stared out through the glass in the door. All I could see through the darkness was the occasional headlight on the highway. As I gazed dumbfounded at the periodic lonely car, I thought I saw a shadow cross the highway. Squinting to search the area, I convinced myself that my mind was just playing tricks on me. After rubbing my eyes to clear them, I checked again, and there was that shadow in the dark again. It had to be him. The shadow paced back and forth near the road, debating its next move.

I opened the door and did what any desperate human would do. I

yelled, "Toby, come. Toby, please come!" He did what every panicked dog would do: He disappeared into the darkness. So much for that well-orchestrated plan. I was going to have to do much better than that.

I went back in and sat down in my chair. Evidently, he had some interest in returning to the scene of the crime. He may have been looking for the last place he had seen Miss Sloan, especially since he wasn't at all acquainted with the area. The poor guy didn't know where else to look for a familiar face. I would have to take advantage of this interest in order to recapture him. All I could think was what they would do on those Animal Planet shows in a similar situation. Then it hit me. I remembered a particular show where wildlife officers had used beefsteak laced with sedatives to help them capture a trouble-some bear that was looting a campground at night. I didn't have access to or a budget for steaks, but there was plenty of canned dog food in the clinic, and bottles full of doggie downers. It was time to attempt to outsmart Toby. I figured he had to be hungry after toying with us in the subdivision earlier. As long as Toby was near the clinic, it was worth a try. Just as I was about to set my trap, the phone rang.

This was a long time before caller ID, but I knew there was about a fifty-fifty chance that it would be Miss Sloan, checking up on Toby. After debating for the first three rings, I grabbed the receiver just before the call transferred over to the answering service.

"Hello, this is Dr. Wells," I said cautiously. After a slightly longer-than-normal pause, the female voice on the other end replied, "How's my Toby? I wondered if I could still pick him up tonight."

She was assuming that Toby was safely tucked back into the clinic and I was just hanging out, waiting for her call. How I wished that were the case. I realized I would have to pick my words very carefully now. Clearing my throat, I said, "Toby is doing fine. He is still out-side, but I am sure he will be coming in soon."

Another hesitation on the other end, then: "You mean he is in one of the dog runs outside?" asked Miss Sloan.

"Well, not exactly. We still haven't caught him." I hated to admit it. "But I am sure that I will have him inside any minute now."

I was afraid that she would want to come in and help me capture the elusive pup, but she acknowledged she was under the influence of painkillers and would not be able to drive safely to the clinic to help me right then. She would be there first thing in the morning, however. Trying to help me that night would have been just an additional liability, especially if she was a little dopey.

I ended the conversation by saying, "Call before you come in tomorrow"—just in case things didn't turn out as I had planned.

Now it was time to get back to coaxing Toby into the clinic. I opened several cans of dog food and placed equal amounts in three food dishes, one for each door of the clinic. Then, after carefully positioning several yellow pills deep inside the food so Toby could not easily spot them, I set a dish in front of each door. The clock behind the reception desk showed it was almost 10:00 P.M. when I kicked back in the chair underneath it to wait for Toby.

A scratch on the front door jolted me out of my slumber. I tripped over myself in my half-conscious rush to the door and dropped onto the linoleum floor. After struggling to my feet in a combination of sleepiness and head-trauma daze, I squinted to focus on the clock only a foot in front of me. It read somewhere in the vicinity of midnight. Another scratch at the front door helped to remind me where I was. I opened the door, and there was Toby in a sedated stupor below me. The pride of escaping us earlier in the day was gone. He no longer held his head in defiance. Now his nose scraped the ground and his tail was literally between his legs. Without hesitation, he stumbled through the open door and collapsed onto the floor. He put his brown head between his paws and looked up at me with half-open eyes.

"Come on, big guy," I whispered as I helped him stand as best he could. Then I escorted him to the nearest kennel in the back room. It was a bit like helping a drunk get to his bed.

He nestled in on top of the old blanket I had placed inside for him, immediately giving in to sleep. The trick worked well, I thought as I gathered up the remaining drug-laced dog food in front of the other two doorways. I didn't want to have a pile of doped-up coyotes sprawled in front of the clinic in the morning, or, worse yet, a mountain lion. In the meantime, I had taken the opportunity to clean out Toby's ears and fill the swollen red canals with soothing medication.

The next day, I arrived early to explain the situation to everyone and call Miss Sloan. "Yes, he is going to be just fine. . . . No, we didn't have to dart him." I did not feel the need to fill her in on the swingset incident. "Yes, he will have to be at the county shelter for ten days to be observed for rabies before you can take him home," I continued.

That was the law in this situation. If the accused does not show any clinical signs of rabies within ten days of the incident, then he can be assumed not to have the disease and will be released. For those who have never seen *Old Yeller,* the clinical signs in dogs can involve aggressive behavior, excessive salivation, and/or neurological problems.

I had no sooner hung up the phone than Lorraine was yelling to the back, "Johnny from Animal Control on the line." I knew this call was coming.

"Doc, you got him alive? How'd you do it?" Johnny was practically begging to know.

"It was just my irresistible personality," I replied, teasing him. "Come get him while he is still a little groggy," I added, hanging up the phone before he had a chance for rebuttal.

In actuality, I did want him to take Toby to the shelter right away.

The dog was doing fine, but I did want to take advantage of his hangover. No sense in waiting for him to get back to full strength, increasing the chance of another one of us getting bitten.

During Toby's incarceration, no signs of rabies were noted. In fact, Johnny had taken this opportunity to socialize him. When I arrived on release day to administer Toby's rabies shot, Johnny held him quietly on a leash, petting him gently as I gave the vaccine.

When we finished, I made the mistake of asking, "How did you change his attitude so quickly, Johnny?"

He had been waiting for me to ask, and he replied smugly, "Oh, Doc, it was just my irresistible personality!"

No Friends' Pets

Almost every veterinarian will tell you that treating a friend's or family member's pet is always high-risk. The chances of something going wrong in this situation are almost 100 percent. There is no scientific reason why it should be this way; it just always seems to happen. The other problem is that it is very hard to say no to people whom you know. They always use lines like "You are the only one we trust," or "We know that you really care about our pet." How is one supposed to respond to this? You probably are somewhat attached to their animal and to them, making it extra hard to send them away. This attachment is exactly why you should say no, because when something goes wrong, the whole relationship is affected. The result can mean the end of a friendship or alienating a relative (which, come to think of it, is not always bad). This is why I should have said no when my old college friend asked me to look at his cat.

Jon and I had been roommates in college. I was doing my prevet training while he was studying prelaw. Jon was a tall, blond, Nordic-looking fellow from northern Iowa. He came from a Scandinavian farming family and always returned from breaks with great pastries that his mother had made for all of us. Jon met his future wife at Iowa State during his freshman year. Kristina was a beautiful girl with brown hair, a sweet smile, and the kind of personality that made everyone she met feel like they were somehow special. They made a great couple, always having fun together, and it rubbed off on the people around them.

The two of them eventually got married and headed for law school out of state, while I started veterinary school. A few years later, I found that they were living in Colorado, too, and we started getting together occasionally. Before I was married, it was especially worth the fifty-five-minute drive to see them when a home-cooked meal was involved. We would sit around their living room, reminiscing and laughing about the great times we'd had in college. It wasn't until the third trip that I even realized they had a pet. That evening, Jon perked up just before I headed out the door.

"Hey, I need to ask you a question about our cat."

"Cat?" I responded, looking a little baffled, I'm sure. "I didn't know you had a cat."

"Yeah, she hides in the basement when people come over. She's not overly agreeable with strangers," he added.

Not traits that made me want to jump right into the caretaker role with this particular feline, but they were old friends and I had just had a free meal. After putting my coat back down on the chair, I asked the loaded question: "What seems to be the problem?"

It turned out to be a good one. Jon was happy to go into a dissertation of what had been going on with their beloved feline.

"It started out when we noticed Bootsy was dragging her butt across the carpet. She got herself in a sitting position, back feet pointed forward, not touching the ground, with her tail limply in tow. It seemed

she was trying to get the most direct pressure possible on her anus."
He continued: "She would then pull herself along with her front legs,
leaving a thin brown stain on the carpet as she went. It sounds kind of
funny, but she almost had a look of satisfaction on her face."

Kristina chimed in at this point. "We didn't want to bother you,
so we took her to the veterinarian down the street. She said that
Bootsy had anal-gland problems and we would either have to have
them emptied every so often or have them removed."

Anal glands are small sacs set just inside the anus of some animals.
They normally produce a watery, odiferous substance that is carried
from the sacs into the rectum through tiny tubes, then released out
into the world through the anus. They can be used to mark territory in
the wild when working properly. They can also be completely emptied
all over an exam-room when a dog or cat becomes stressed. In a
skunk, these are the same glands that release the famous smell we all
recognize. These little sacs can cause a problem for the animal when
the connecting tubes to the rectum become clogged and the glands
get backed up. They can even develop into abscesses. You can imagine the discomfort to the animal, which explains why they drag their
behinds to try to release the pressure. Thank goodness humans don't
have them. Just the thought brings some bad visuals to mind.

Back to Bootsy. This was the point where one of Jon's old quirks
came through. Some might say it was a Scandinavian trait, but Jon
was extremely tight. Even though he was now an attorney who was
making a very good living, he still didn't want to spend cash that he
didn't absolutely have to.

"It costs fifty bucks every time we take her in, and it takes only a
few minutes," he blurted. "If we have the glands removed, they said,
it would be a minimum of eight hundred!" His face was getting red
just from talking about it. I wanted to ask him what his hourly billing

rate was, but he was a dear old friend, so I held my tongue. Kristina calmed him down; then we headed for the basement to find the infamous Bootsy.

Their basement was standard suburban issue: white painted drywall and a tan Berber carpet. Well, tan, with a few dark brown streaks. There was a television surrounded by overstuffed couches at one end and a wet bar for parties at the other. Bootsy's well-kept litter box was positioned next to the wall, not far from the bar, but there was no sign of Bootsy.

Kristina called for her reclusive pet. "Bootsy, here, kitty, kitty, kitty. Where are you hiding? We need to take a look at you." Jon and I stood quietly so as not to startle the worried cat.

Kristina repeated her call and was finally answered by a meek *meow* from under a couch. The cat had reluctantly given away her position. Kristina lay facedown on the floor, talking to Bootsy quietly while cautiously reaching her right hand under the couch.

"Okay, Bootsy, now come out and let Dr. Jeff take a look at you. He just wants to help you feel better."

Bootsy actually believed her human. She appeared through the skirting at the bottom of the couch. She was a little black cat with the appropriate four white sock feet. Kristina picked her up, holding her against her chest, stroking her quietly while Jon and I waited for the appropriate time to advance. Kristina eventually gave us the nod and we moved in, softly encouraging Bootsy as we approached. I rubbed her head, trying to build up her trust.

"It's okay, girl, no big deal. You've had this done before." As I said it, I realized that was probably not the best line to use.

Bootsy kept her green eyes on me, following my every move. She had been through this before, but so far, her torturer hadn't actually shown up in her own home. I sent Jon upstairs for some tissue. If I

had been warned that I would be doing this procedure, I would have brought some latex gloves with me, but tissues would have to do. Jon reappeared, handing me the tissue, and I worked my way down Bootsy's back, heading for the target.

"Nice Bootsy. Easy, Bootsy" was all I could think of to say.

When I reached her tail, I raised it slightly to expose the problem area. This caused Bootsy to warn me with a guttural growl, as if to say, If you continue with this, things are going to go badly for you. Despite the warning, I grasped her tail with my left hand and headed in with the tissues. Bootsy stiffened her back legs, and Kristina drew her in even more tightly. The directions for anal-gland emptying go something like this: Squeeze with thumb and forefinger at approximately four and eight o'clock. I had done this many times on an exam table with a trained technician holding the patient, but not in a suburban basement. I knew the potential for human injury was high, yet I didn't want to disappoint my old friends. I had to get the job done. Pressing the tissue against the appropriate spots, I squeezed. At first, nothing happened; then when I applied a little more pressure, the glands released their brown fluid, one of the nastiest-smelling substances nature has to offer. Unfortunately for me, the tissue didn't act as much of a barrier, and the contents leaked onto my fingers.

Bootsy decided that she'd had enough, and she leaped from Kristina's arms, causing them only minimal damage. She retreated to her hideout under the couch again, where she growled in protest until we headed upstairs. We had accomplished our task and no one had to go to the emergency room.

"Oh, thank you so much. She was so good for you," Kristina said as she gave me a hug. "And all it cost us was a dinner," Jon chimed in.

Their enthusiasm waned when they got a whiff of the odor wafting off my fingers, and they pointed me toward the bathroom. Three rounds of hand washing didn't even make a dent in the unrelenting fragrance. It would be stuck on my hands for at least twenty-four hours, making me socially unacceptable for that time period. Keeping my hands in my pockets, I thanked my hosts and let myself out, leaving them with that "just ate a lemon" look on their faces.

Jon let me clear the house by a few yards, then yelled, "We'll have you back again in about six weeks! You may want to bring gloves."

I didn't really want to become Bootsy's personal anal-gland emptier, but Kristina was a great cook and they were a lot of fun.

Six weeks later, I was back enjoying another great meal, but this time I had a pair of latex gloves in my back pocket. It took just a little longer for Kristina to catch Bootsy this time, and the feline was a bit more testy about the procedure. Kristina's wounds were more severe this round.

Over the next year, there were several more dinners, followed by Bootsy's treatments, each a little more painful for all of us. I knew we were getting closer to needing a more permanent fix for Bootsy's renegade glands. Things culminated one day when Kristina got hold of me at the clinic.

"I'm afraid we need to have an emergency dinner," she warned me. "Bootsy has some bloody discharge coming from her, well, area. Could you come down tonight and take a look?"

After pizza and a safari to find Bootsy in the basement, I was able to sneak a peek at the problem. Sure enough, the left anal gland had become infected, breaking through the skin when the pressure got to be too much.

"Is she going to be okay?" Kristina asked.

"It should be fine after some flushing and antibiotics, but I think we are at the point where we should discuss removing the glands. They are going to get nothing but worse," I said.

Kristina looked a little concerned at the thought of surgery. Forehead wrinkled and eyebrows raised, Jon, on the other hand, couldn't resist asking, "So, how much will this set me back?" This comment translated to "How big a break will I get for being a friend?"

With much objection, Bootsy eventually let me flush the abscessed anal gland with some diluted hydrogen peroxide in a syringe. Then I grabbed some kitty antibiotics out of the truck and popped them in an unsuspecting Bootsy's mouth before she could figure out what I was up to. The secret about cats and antibiotic pills is that the first one is the easiest. After they know what is coming and have time to mount a defense, the job gets almost impossible. It is easy for the veterinarian to leave instructions for the owner to give one pill twice a day, knowing all too well that humans will be put at risk. It is a little harder just to hand off the pills and run when the recipients have your home phone number. The upside was that I knew the surgery would sound like a better idea after a week of convincing Bootsy to take the pills. After a trip to the doctor's office for wounds on Jon's hands, they were ready to bring their kitty up for surgery.

On Monday morning, they were waiting on the clinic's doorstep when Christie arrived to open up. By the time I showed up, Bootsy had already drawn blood. I found Christie standing over the treatment sink, washing out her wounds. She flashed me a less than cordial look, then nodded toward the waiting room, where Jon and Kristina sat patiently. Bootsy was not so patient. She was confined in one of the stainless-steel cages in the back room and her objecting low growl could be heard in every room of the building. I walked into the waiting room.

"Hey, guys, I see Bootsy's all checked in and ready to go," which was a lame attempt to lighten the mood on my part.

Kristina's voice was a little shaky. "Are you sure that we are doing the right thing? I'm so worried about her."

I started to answer, when Jon added, "If we keep this up, one of us is going to end up in the hospital. We have to go through with this for our safety and Bootsy's sanity."

I nodded my head in agreement. Thank goodness Jon had fielded that question. I couldn't have said it better or more convincingly. Jon put his arm around Kristina's waist and they headed for the door. I told them I would call when the surgery was over, closing the waiting room door behind them.

Christie met me back in the treatment area. She had her left index finger wrapped with some white medical tape.

"I don't know how you're going to restrain that cat, but I don't plan on taking any more hits," she said with her teeth clenched.

I couldn't let Christie get injured again. I was going to have to be the restrainer. I pulled up the proper amount of anesthetic and handed it to Christie. She managed to eke out a smile, knowing I was the one who would be taking the risk. I dug a thick bath towel out of the laundry pile. With the towel in my left hand, I opened the door of Bootsy's cage with my right.

"Okay, Bootsy, if you let me do this, I won't show up at your house anymore. Or at least I won't chase you around the basement," I whispered while putting the towel over the upset cat.

I kept up the one-way conversation as I slid Bootsy to the back of the stainless box. Once I had the feline pressed up against the back wall, Christie knew to reach in and inject the clear fluid into her back leg. We had been down this road before. Bootsy kept up her distinctive growl during the whole thing, yet she made no attempt to inflict human injury.

Eventually, the growl began to wane and Bootsy dropped off into anesthetic sleep. Christie placed her carefully on the table, prepping her for surgery. I scrubbed up and began the tedious task of removing the tiny glands that were causing so many problems for all of us. After ligating the ducts that connected the glands to the rectum, I teased out the stinky little sacs, doing everything possible to be sure there was minimal contamination. The contents of the glands would obviously not be something you would want to leave behind in the incision. The other complication to avoid during this surgery is damaging any of the surrounding nerves. Mistakenly cutting through one of these could possibly lead to fecal incontinence—probably a friendship breaker.

After I had the glands out, Christie flushed the holes left behind with saline before I sutured them closed. The surgery went as well as could be expected—no major complications.

As Bootsy woke up on top of a heating pad, I called her parents to relieve their fears. The next morning, Bootsy was back to normal, or at least normal for Bootsy. The offending anal glands were gone, but the growl was not. Christie was more than glad to have Kristina remove Bootsy from her confines to avoid any combative contact. Everyone went home happy.

I called and talked to Kristina the next day. "Bootsy is doing great. She's got a great appetite and is just as testy as normal," she said happily.

I felt pretty good about myself. Everyone seemed to be pleased, even Bootsy. But then on Friday morning, Lorraine told me that Kristina was on the phone.

Kristina's voice quivered. "Bootsy isn't doing so well. Her surgery area seems to be really bothering her. Can you come down and take a look?" This invite did not appear to include dinner. I knew I should not have done work for friends and should have referred them to another competent veterinary surgeon in the area instead.

I left the clinic as early as I could and arrived at Bootsy's house just as Jon was getting home. Kristina already had Bootsy in her arms. She had been easy to catch and seemed to be less disagreeable than usual. She even let me take her temperature with a rectal thermometer, a humiliation she never would have put up with if she'd been feeling at all normal. Bootsy's temperature was elevated—104 degrees Fahrenheit. Sure enough, the left incision was leaking a small amount of pus. Bootsy had developed an infection.

"Is she going to be okay?" Kristina asked cautiously. I assured her that Bootsy would live; we would just have to do a couple things to make sure she healed properly.

I clipped one of the sutures out, allowing the pus to drain. After putting together a bottle of antibiotics, I popped one down Bootsy and left the rest for them to give her over the course of the next week, knowing full well that, as before, this would get harder to do as the week wore on.

Bootsy improved quickly. Kristina kept me informed on a daily basis. Even Jon noticed that her attitude was improving. I seemed to have dodged the bullet on this one. In six months, I was invited back for dinner. Bootsy even came upstairs, occasionally rubbing up against my leg.

Jon noticed her unprovoked affection. "She's been a different cat since the surgery. She's got a whole new attitude. I guess I would have been a little less than agreeable if I'd had an anal-gland issue."

I laughed, but I was quietly thinking the same thing to myself. The ramifications would be endless.

Horns and Hair

The Hansberger ranch was in South Park. I had driven by it before but had never actually been called out to see an animal
there. The ranch sat on the high-mountain meadow that makes up
most of the South Park area. South Park consists of miles of flat grass-
lands surrounded by rugged snowcapped peaks. The setting was so
beautiful, it was almost hard to believe it was real. On a clear day, the
mountains sparkled like diamonds and you could see for thirty miles
in every direction. On a bad day, with the snow blowing horizontally,
you were lucky if you could see the front of your vehicle from the
driver's seat. This day was one of the good ones.

I had been called out to see a sick calf. Lorraine had relayed the
message when I'd showed up at the clinic that morning. "They had
been using a vet from somewhere north of them, but he has not been
returning their calls. So they have decided to give you a try." I, of
course, jumped at the chance to take a drive to their ranch on a gor-
geous Colorado day in mid-February.

I pulled into the ranch driveway, swung open the metal gate, and rumbled over the cattle guard. A welcoming committee of six golden retrievers greeted me. They barked at the truck, then followed me the rest of the way up the driveway, tails wagging. The house was a big weathered two-story building covered in white paint chips holding on for dear life. Behind the house were three huge barns built from massive logs, bigger than any found in the vicinity today. The ranch had at one time been a train stop. The Hansberger barns had been used to house horses and cattle on the way to and from Denver. The original corrals still stood, surrounding the massive structures.

The entire homestead had been built over a hundred years before by some of the original settlers. Rumor had it that when the first ranchers moved into the region, the landscape was still speckled with the remnants of Native American tepees. The Ute tribe once used the area for their summer hunting grounds. Now the huge barns themselves were reminders of times gone by, when the ranches had huge herds of cattle grazing their land. By now, most of the water rights had been sold off and the herds had shrunk to a fraction of their former size.

I pulled up to the front door of the old house and unfolded myself out of the truck just as the owners appeared in the doorway. A young girl, followed by her mother, a medium-height blond woman in her mid-thirties. They were dressed well for the wind, wearing heavy jackets and stocking caps. Their sunglasses were nearly as big as ski goggles, and their snow pants were stuffed into heavy insulated leather boots with thick treads. Both were properly dressed for a day in South Park, where even on a clear day the wind could blow right through you if you didn't have the proper attire.

The mother seemed genuinely happy that I had showed up, yet her daughter appeared to be more of a skeptic.

Looking me up and down, she croaked, "How long have you been out of school?"

I was a little taken aback by the question. I thought for a minute, not wanting to give her the impression I might have had less experience than the previous practitioner. "Long enough," I finally replied. She didn't like that at all, flashing me a little-girl look of disapproval. She was nine going on twenty-five.

We headed for the pen that held the sick calf. Before we got there, Mrs. Hansberger brought up an interesting point, one that should have clued me in. "You may want to bring any medicine or tools you might need with you. It's usually best to have everything to use at once." I just assumed that she didn't want me to have to make a lot of trips back to the truck. I took her advice and went back to gather necessities. I stuffed my pockets with antibiotics, syringes, a thermometer, and a stethoscope and ran back to catch up with them at the corral. This was where the sick calf had been separated from the rest until it could be treated.

To my surprise, the calf was a Scottish Highlander, a breed I had seen only in pictures or at livestock fairs. Across the fence, on the opposite side of where I was standing, was the rest of the herd. About seventy-five pairs of eyes mostly covered with hairy bangs stared back at me. They seemed to be watching over the sick calf, and I was the guy they were worried about. Highlanders are a longhaired, shaggy breed of cattle and have long horns that curl up at the tip for maximum "spearing" capabilities. They look like a cross between a buffalo and a yak, two animals with which I'd had some previous experience. Highlanders are immigrants from Scotland, designed for surviving the extreme conditions of the Highlands—hence the name. These same traits also gave them an advantage here in South Park. At ten thousand feet above sea level, sharing space with bears and mountain lions, they were still in good shape.

Drawing my attention back to the calf and away from the watchful eyes of the herd, Mrs. Hansberger began giving me the history of the calf's illness. "He's about two weeks old, and I noticed a couple days ago that he was dragging a little behind the rest of the group. It took me a little longer to get him separated off than I had hoped. Harry wouldn't even let me get close for almost two days."

After picking up on the blank look on my face, she explained that Harry was the large black steer standing in the middle of the herd. He was the one with horns twice as long and tall as those on any of the others. The story goes that after Harry was neutered, the Hansbergers held on to him because of his important role in the herd. He had positioned himself as the official nursemaid and protector of the young calves. Harry had even been known to use his horns to help weak calves stand up and get moving after they were born. He would slide one of his mammoth horns under the belly of the calf, lifting it onto its feet until it could start to walk. If he protected the calves from the Hansbergers, I wondered how he would feel about me. I was also having some concerns about why the previous veterinarian was not returning their calls.

Mrs. Hansberger climbed the high wooden fence and dropped into the pen with the calf. I followed behind, while her daughter, Holly, stayed perched on the top board. A small brown woolly calf with large brown eyes lay tucked into a sheltered part of the fence. Its hair was soft and fluffy, not yet matted from age and seasons in South Park. I instinctively wanted to walk over and scratch his belly.

Mrs. Hansberger easily slipped a halter on the lethargic little guy and together we got him tied to a nearby post. He was less than happy about being restrained for the first time in his life, but I was still able to listen to his lungs. By the time I got a rectal temperature, he was beginning to put up a real fuss, throwing himself around like a fish on the end of a line. Calves that are distressed make a *moo* noise that sounds more like a bawling baby, alerting their mothers that they might need some help. His lungs crackled and wheezed when I listened with the stethoscope, and his temperature was almost 105 degrees, all typical signs of pneumonia. I was aware this would be the only time we might get this calf alone, so I pulled up a syringeful of long-acting antibiotic and injected its thick contents into the calf's hip.

Suddenly, Holly began yelling from her fence top. "Mom, they're coming around, they're coming around!" While I was concentrating on the sick calf, I hadn't noticed that the rest of the herd had disappeared.

"We need to go! Are you almost done?" Mrs. Hansberger said in a nervous tone.

"Well, I really need to give him another antibiotic orally," I replied as I rifled through my pockets for the large oval-shaped tablet I had brought from the truck. It wasn't in my pants pockets. Maybe in my coat?

Holly sounded off again. "Mom, they're getting closer. Mom!"

"We've got to go. We've just got to go!" Mrs. Hansberger said impatiently.

I didn't understand what the big deal was. There were plenty of fences between us and the well-armed herd. What I didn't understand was that one of the gates, about a half a mile away, had so much snow drifted up against it that the Hansbergers couldn't get it closed. The Highlanders, with their uncanny, primal sense of self-preservation, knew where it was. While I was doctoring the calf, they had run away from us to get to the open gate and were now coming back through the opening on our side to save their calf. The other thing I didn't realize was that Highlanders are unlike other breeds of cattle, in that the herd truly functions as one. It wasn't just the calf's mother that was upset about the calf; it was the *entire* herd. I finally felt the large pill in my coat pocket. Scrambling with the plastic dispensing device, I placed the pill in the proper end and attempted to get the

entire thing in the calf's mouth. The frustrated calf rejected the idea, flailing back and forth against his halter.

Mrs. Hansberger was now yelling at me. "Run, we have to run now!"

At the last minute, the calf opened his mouth just enough for me to get the pill dispenser in. The second the calf swallowed, Mrs. Hansberger pulled a pocketknife from her coat and cut the rope, setting the little guy free. By now, we could hear the hoofbeats. We turned and ran for the fence. It was only about ten yards away, but it felt like miles. Mrs. Hansberger was a few steps ahead of me, which was only fair, since I had been holding up the show. Only a few more strides and I would be at the fence. I could feel them behind me now, breathing and snorting. They were inside the corral, right on our heels. I fought the urge to look back to see how close they were. I knew that the fraction of a second I wasted might be the one that got me killed.

Mrs. Hansberger made the fence, vaulting herself over. Holly let out a gleeful scream upon her mother's escape. Only two more steps and I would be there. By the time my right foot hit the first board on the fence, I could swear I felt warm breath on the back of my neck. Grabbing the top board with both hands, I launched my Carhartt-clad self into the air. The next few seconds were spent in that fog between life and death. Time tends to get stuck in slow motion when you don't know how it will all end. I slammed to the ground, anticipating a hoof in my back. Gasping, I looked up, to see Harry staring down at me . . . through the boards of the fence. It was the ground that had knocked the wind out of me. I had made it over and now lay on my back on the safe side. It was a bed of ice and snow, but I was ecstatic to be on it. I had no gaping chest wound. Harry raked his horns up and down the boards of the fence to emphasize his anger. The resulting noise sounded like a kid dragging a stick along a picket fence, amplified tenfold.

Mrs. Hansberger, recovered from her scramble over the fence, was now standing over me, looking less than pleased. "Next time I tell you to run, RUN!" she blurted as she turned and stomped off.

I heard Holly ask, "Is he going to be all right?"

"Oh, he'll be fine. He's younger and faster than the last one," her mother chirped.

I was still on the ground, with Harry and his harem gawking at me through the fence. Other cows tended to the calf, reassuringly nuzzling him with their shaggy heads. I began the process of standing up slowly, making sure that all my parts worked as I went. A couple of the dogs started licking my face to encourage me. The only thing broken was the glass antibiotic bottle in my back pocket. There went the profit.

I picked the glass out of my pocket and a few pieces out of myself. Mrs. Hansberger had already disappeared into the house, and Holly was headed that way.

Holly yelled at me on her way to the door. "Come on in, figure up the bill, and Mom will pay you." I grabbed a blank receipt, then headed for the front door. In the kitchen, Mrs. Hansberger and Holly sat at the table, Mrs. Hansberger with the ranch checkbook lying in front of her. The golden retrievers were by now scattered over the floor, making it a little tough to maneuver around the kitchen to pull up a chair. Mrs. Hansberger motioned to the one closest to me. I sat down gently and wrote up the bill, sliding it over to Mrs. Hansberger. She looked at it, nodding her head. After writing the check, she headed into the pantry, coming back with a pan of brownies. She proceeded to cut a big piece for each of us, even wrapping up an extra one in paper towel for me to take home. Before the brownies, I was working on excuses for why I could never come back. Now, I was beginning to reconsider. Little did I know it was the first of dozens of times that I would sit at this table, write up a bill, and enjoy Mrs. Hansberger's baking. Luckily, this would be the only time I would have a sore backside from recently removed glass, but not the last time I would be pursued by the Highlanders.

Side Effects

The last thing they tell you as you are graduating from veterinary school is "Do no harm." It seems simple enough, but it can be harder to live up to than one might think. As veterinarians, we always have the best intentions in regard to helping the patient, but once in a while things happen that are just completely beyond one's control. There are certain procedures that have more potential for unwittingly doing harm, such as major surgeries on older animals, but there are days when nothing should go wrong. On one such day, every appointment I had was routine—a goat neuter, some vaccinations, and a deworming. Not a lot of potential for problems, or so I thought.

The last appointment of the afternoon was actually with two separate clients who lived right next to each other. They both had horses, and today they were to get their spring vaccinations. I wanted Christie to go with me to help things go smoothly, making it easier to get done at a decent time. There where six horses and one burro between the two clients.

"You bet, I would love to get out of the office today," Christie yipped. "What time do we head out?"

I let her know that the appointment was at 3:00 P.M., so we would need to leave by about 2:30.

"Sounds good," she said, getting on with her morning with a little more spring in her step.

I didn't take her with me on large-animal calls as often as she wanted to go. Most of the time there was more need for her at the clinic, but occasionally I really needed her assistance outside. She always seemed to appreciate it and was just happy to get out in the fresh air. At 2:30, we jumped in the truck, which was loaded with horse vaccine and dewormer. We knew both of the clients and their animals fairly well. There shouldn't be any big surprise, I thought. I had been to both places several times, and no one had tried to kick or bite me, not even the owners.

We were instructed to pull into the Winstons' place first. Mrs. Winston had three children, all of whom had piano lessons later that day, so they needed to leave by 4:00 P.M. Mrs. Winston was a tall, thin, businesslike woman for whom every step had a purpose. She had to be this way in order to manage the kids, ages two, four, and six. Even though they demanded nearly every second of every day, she still maintained a good attitude and even found time for her horses.

"Oh, I'm so glad you guys made it on time," she said with a smile. "These kids are at a tough age. The youngest wasn't planned, you know."

We nodded as we walked through the small gate into the area where the horses were kept. She had been explaining the unplanned one since the first day I met her. Mrs. Winston usually went on to explain how they loved the youngest child just as much as the other two. But he must have been acting up on this day. The three children lined up on the outside of the fence, a safe place to watch the festivities. They were quiet and happy for now because Mrs. Winston had provided each with a box of animal crackers—a savvy mother.

She already had all five horses tied to individual pine trees within the corral. It was great to have a client who was so organized. Too often, we had to help the owner chase his or her animals for half an hour before we could begin looking them over.

"Thanks for having them all ready to go for us," I said to her.

"I have to be organized; otherwise, my entire life would fall apart," Mrs. Winston replied proudly. "With these kids and all their activities, it's like running a small corporation."

"We'll get the horses done so that you can get the kids to their piano lessons," Christie chimed in.

I guessed that she, too, had something going later that day. Unlike Mrs. Winston, however, she kept her private life fairly private, so I didn't say anything.

We began working our way through the small herd, examining each horse, vaccinating them and squirting deworming paste into their mouths. But we had an extra helper we hadn't planned on, one that didn't really speed up the process, but actually slowed us down a little. The uninvited assistant was the Winston's two-year-old Siberian husky, Hattie. The young dog was sweet and playful, but she wanted to be involved in everything we were doing. The corral had not only been fenced for horses but was also covered with wire dog fence to keep her inside. She jumped on Christie, trying to grab syringes to play with. I could see Christie's frustration level rising as her clean pants and baby blue smock took on a paw-print design.

"Stay down! If you don't knock it off, I'm going to give you a shot," she growled.

Now I knew for sure Christie had plans later and didn't want to have to change her clothes before going out.

"I'm so sorry," Mrs. Winston said. "She just wants to play. Hattie thinks that the horses are her pack. We don't have any other dogs, so they are her only friends."

I could tell this wasn't good enough for Christie. Afraid that she might say something we would regret later, I decided to intervene.

"Oh, we're used to it," I interjected. "We'd rather dogs be friendly than try to bite us. Right, Christie?"

She nodded in reluctant agreement, flashed me one of her looks, and went back to pulling up vaccine, with Hattie's assistance. Even with Hattie bouncing around them, the horses were just as well behaved as expected.

We finished the last horse within our one-hour time frame. Packing up our empty syringes and paste worming tubes, we walked toward the gate, with Hattie still trying to steal a potential toy. I pushed open the fence while explaining to Mrs. Winston about how she could expect the horses to act after their vaccines. I was not paying enough attention to my surroundings, and Hattie took advantage, slipping her narrow body through the open gate. Huskies are natural runners, so once she gained her freedom, she was off.

"Oh crap," fretted Mrs. Winston. "When she gets out, she's impossible to catch."

"I'm so sorry," I said sheepishly.

"It's okay," she responded; "I should have warned you that Hattie would attempt to escape. She does it all the time. She'll come back in a couple hours. Always does."

Christie gave me a smirk, as if to say, How do you feel about Hattie now, smart guy? Then she turned back toward the truck with a new air of confidence about her. Mrs. Winston, the kids, and I made a couple feeble attempts to catch Hattie, with absolutely no luck. Hattie just seemed to laugh at us as she darted around the yard.

"She'll be home by dark. No need to worry," Mrs. Winston promised as she loaded the kids into her Suburban.

I was really going to feel bad if something happened to Hattie. As a veterinarian, you always have a list of horrid possibilities running through your head when a dog goes for an unchaperoned tour. It could be hit by a car, shot by an angry neighbor, or attacked by coyotes. The list of life-threatening possibilities goes on and on. I had seen these unfortunate canines come into the clinic all too often.

Christie smiled at me from the passenger side of the truck. She knew I was worried, and her expression seemed more genuine now. She even tried to comfort me.

"Hattie will be all right. Mrs. Winston said she's done this before."

"Hope you are right," I said with doubt in my voice.

I drove the truck down the driveway and cut onto the main road, then made an immediate left into the next-door neighbor's drive. Mrs. Potts was the one sharing the call charge with Mrs. Winston. She had a horse and a burro scheduled for routine vaccinations and deworming.

Mrs. Potts was a small, happy woman with long blond hair framing her big blue eyes. She was about thirty-five years old and had with no children, except for her horse, Oreo, and her burro, Missy. She had acquired Missy to keep Oreo company, but she loved both of them equally. She could often be seen riding Oreo down the back roads, with Missy in tow. She would tie Missy's lead rope to Oreo's saddle horn and off they would go. She didn't want Missy to miss out on anything by being left behind. She kept their pen spotless, while consistently feeding them just a little more than they really needed. On this particular day, she had gotten off work early so she could meet us.

"You don't think the vaccinations will have any side effects, do you?" Mrs. Potts asked cautiously.

She was a bit of a worrier when it came to her babies. She continued: "I've heard that they can get stiff, even go off of their feed, or worse."

I assured her that it was rare that we ever had a problem, seemingly muting her concerns for now.

Mrs. Potts had already caught Missy, so we started with her. I vaccinated her for the common equine virus and dewormed her with the same broad-spectrum oral paste that we had used on the Winstons' herd. Sometimes burros can be a little tough to work on, especially if they don't receive a lot of time and attention from their owners. Abnormally strong for their size and with a low center of gravity, uncooperative burros can be formidable adversaries. More than one has dragged me around a corral with a syringe in my hand. Missy, on the other hand, was the perfect patient. Christie took the halter off, letting Missy go, when Hattie showed up. Scooting under a loose spot in the fence, she popped out into the corral with us. This wouldn't appear to be a big deal, except for the fact that many burros hate dogs. It seems to be some kind of deep-rooted, primitive reaction to eliminate the potential predator. The instinct is so strong that ranchers will put burros in with their sheep or cattle to run off stray dogs and coyotes. Missy was no exception. Her primal drive kicked into gear and she took off after Hattie in a crazed fury. Her single mission in life became to destroy Hattie. The two of them tore around the enclosure, Missy with teeth bared as she tried to stomp Hattie with her front feet. At one point, Missy's hooves made contact with Hattie's back, knocking her down in a cloud of dust and whimpers. Mrs. Potts was frantic.

"Stop it, both of you!" she screamed. "Hattie, get out, now!"

But it didn't do any good. Missy was possessed and Hattie was too panicked to find an exit. Great, the Winstons' dog was about to be killed and I was the one who had let her out to begin with. Finally, after a couple of minutes, which felt like a stressful eternity, Christie and I were able to get between the two, giving Hattie just enough time to find an exit and make a beeline for home. No harm, no foul. Both dog and burro had survived. Even Mrs. Potts started to calm down, just in time to get worked up again.

Missy walked over to the far end of the pen and lay down. She began sweating profusely, then started to roll in the dirt, the classic signs of abdominal pain or colic. Since horses and burros don't have the ability to vomit, intestinal cramps are not as easily remedied as they are for humans.

"What is going on with Missy?" Mrs. Potts asked with a tremor in her voice. "Why is she acting that way?"

I would have answered, but I really wasn't sure. The catalyst had to have been Hattie. The stress of chasing her around the pen must have caused her intestines to stop moving food through and to shut down. I looked at Christie. She raised her eyebrows and gave me that "I have no clue" look. She handed me Missy's halter and I slipped it back on over the burro's head. One of the first things to do for colic is to get the animal up and walking, so that's what I attempted to do. Sometimes this will get the intestines moving again.

"Come on, Missy, let's get up and walk this off," I said as I pulled against the lead rope to get her up. I wanted to say, Get up now! Please don't die.

But I tried to keep my cool, not letting Mrs. Potts in on the severity of the situation. Christie came to my assistance, pushing on Missy's back end until she reluctantly lifted herself to her feet. The poor thing was unsteady and still more interested in lying back down than in staying up. Christie took over on the front end, pulling Missy along, while I ran for something to give the burro for pain relief.

Trying to find a jugular vein on a moving burro who is also trying to lie down would test the skills of even the most experienced veterinarian. An intravenous injection in a burro is a bugger in the best of situations. A burro's skin is thicker than that of most animals, and when a burro tightens up the heavy musculature of its neck, as burros always do when stressed, the vein all but disappears. I walked along beside Missy, searching desperately for the target while holding a syringeful of intestinal relaxant. From Mrs. Pott's angle, it must have looked more like I was performing some kind of acupuncture treatment.

"Do you have to stick her so many times?" Mrs. Potts asked, unable to hold back. She was worried enough about her baby without my making a pincushion out of her.

Just then, I made contact, and we all breathed a sigh of relief. Blood flowed into the syringe, mixing with the clear medication. I pushed the whole thing back into Missy's vein quickly, before losing contact. Christie continued coaxing Missy around the corral and I took over the pushing role.

I kept encouraging the struggling animal. "Come on, Missy, you can do it. You're going to be fine."

In reality, these words were for Mrs. Potts's benefit. She was still standing in the center of the corral, her weepy eyes following Missy's every move. The drug should have kicked in within a few minutes, but it didn't seem to be giving the burro much relief. She wasn't getting worse, but we weren't seeing the improvement we were hoping for, either. Mrs. Potts was getting more upset.

"She isn't getting better, is she?" she asked.

I replied in the best way I thought I could. "Well, she isn't yet, but I am sure she will soon," I said.

I was sure Missy would get better, but I wished she would hurry up and do it.

When we were at the far end of the pen, I whispered to Christie, "If you have any suggestions, don't hold back!"

Christie shook her head, made a dumbfounded face, and responded with a simple "No clue."

I was on my own, and Mrs. Potts was getting more impatient. I could tube Missy with some laxative, but this treatment would not help for hours. We needed a more immediate fix. After all, the whole situation was my fault. I had set the whole thing in motion by letting Hattie out.

As if things weren't bad enough, Missy decided to develop a new symptom. She stuck her tongue out the side of her mouth as far as she could, then forced out a showstopping cough. She did it again and again, repeating the horrible noise every five seconds. Each time, her tongue would jut out about a foot from her mouth, like a frog's lashing out to grab an insect. This coughing spell put Mrs. Potts over the edge.

"What is going on?" she demanded. "Is she going to make it?"

It was time to admit to myself and Mrs. Potts what the cough had confirmed. Missy was having a full-blown anaphylactic reaction. I was sure that this would not have happened if it weren't for the insane dog chase. The vaccine we had given Missy had moved through her body too quickly as she stormed around the corral after Hattie. This reaction most likely had led to the intestinal pain and the inflammation in the lungs and throat, which resulted in this awful cough. Some of the paste dewormer was probably still stuck in Missy's esophagus, making the situation even worse. As far as the question of whether Missy was going to die or not, I really didn't know. When I glanced at Christie, I knew what she was thinking. Each time Missy coughed, it might be the last time. It was way too easy to imagine her collapsing on the ground in a heap. Even with all these mental pictures running through my head, I had to do something about it, while not letting Mrs. Potts know how freaked-out I was.

"She's going to be okay. She's just having a little reaction." I didn't totally believe what I'd just said, but I would have to make it happen now. "I'm going to give her a large dose of cortisone to counteract the reaction," I told her, and ran for the truck.

This time, I knew right where to find the skittish vein, and I forced the medicine through the narrow needle. By now, I couldn't decipher whose sweat was all over my shirt—Missy's, from my rubbing against her, or my own, from being a nervous wreck.

"This should help," I said to Mrs. Potts. "It shouldn't be long and Missy will be as good as new."

"Oh, I hope so. I just can't take much more of this," she whimpered.

I couldn't blame her for being upset. Christie and I continued our ritual of towing Missy around the enclosure.

Eventually, after a long twenty minutes and the disappearance of Mrs. Potts into the house, Missy's coughs became a little less frequent. Her sweating stopped and she ceased trying to lie down. We hadn't noticed that Mrs. Potts had been watching through her kitchen window, coming out only when she was sure Missy was really improving. It took another hour before the ravaged burro stopped coughing entirely.

Christie and I stayed until I was sure the hacking would not resume and Missy took up eating again. Christie was not happy about the delay, but Mrs. Potts let her use the phone twice, keeping her relatively happy. The calls must have appeased whoever was on the other end.

By the time it was over, Christie and I, Mrs. Potts, and especially the burro were all exhausted. We made a mutual decision that I should come back and vaccinate Oreo at a later date so Mrs. Potts wouldn't have another animal to stress over that evening. She was very appreciative.

"Thank you so much for fixing my Missy and staying until she was completely recovered. I could not have handled her in that condition by myself," she said, wiping her brow with her sleeve.

"No problem," I replied, trying to act as if this was the outcome I had expected all along. "I will come by and check on her in the morning. No charge!"

All I could think of was how glad I was that both Missy and Hattie were still with us. I could never have left without knowing if Missy was going to be all right, not to mention Mrs. Potts.

Once Christie and I were back in the truck, we smiled and waved good-bye to Mrs. Potts. Christie spoke through smiling teeth. "What in the heck happened back there? I thought for sure that burro was not going to make it."

"So did I," I responded, and explained my theory of the vaccine reaction.

She agreed that this was a reasonable justification. "Well, don't let it happen again. I can't handle it." She sighed.

About two hours later, I called to check in with Mrs. Potts. I got her husband on the line instead. "She said to tell you that everything is fine. No more coughing, and Missy is still eating. The only problem now is that I am sleeping alone tonight. She has made herself a bed in the barn so she can keep an eye on things." Then he sighed deeply. "I swear, sometimes I think she cares more for those animals than she does for me." That was a whole other issue, one that I was not going to touch. Besides, I had a whole night of coughing-burro dreams to look forward to. Hopefully, Mrs. Winston had gotten Hattie back in her confines. Oh, now I would never sleep!

Dog Attack

Every sheep owner's nightmare is a predator attack on his flock. Since the beginning of time, people have been protecting their livestock from those looking for an easy meal. In the Rocky Mountain region, mountain lions and coyotes are the most obvious assailants. They will usually take one animal out of the flock for a legitimate meal, but the real threat comes from packs of domestic dogs. They are often neighbor's pets that are allowed to run free and hook up for group hunting trips. Dog packs don't typically take out one animal like their wild counterparts; they tend to maim as many as possible. My own sheep were attacked by dogs when I was a boy. It was a horrifying event, one that I will never forget. So my heart sank when Lorraine informed me that Jamie Shultz's small sheep herd had been attacked by dogs during the night. "She said that it was quite a mess and not all of them made it." This would have been a bad situation in any case, but Jamie treated her sheep more like pets than livestock. All of them had names, and she could tell you not only when they were born but who their mothers were. Her husband was the same way. Jamie said he was already cleaning wounds while they waited for me.

Christie followed me out to the truck and plopped down into the passenger seat, uninvited. "You're going to need me for this one," she said with enough determination that I decided not to argue. When you work with someone as closely as we did, that person sometimes knows what is best for you before you do. The Shultz place was about fifteen miles away. The road there curved down through the pines, then followed a river through a small mountain town that time had forgotten. Although it had once been a vibrant railroad town, all that remained were a couple small churches whose congregations had dwindled to a meager few and a general store where nothing, other than the merchandise, had changed since it was built.

The old landmark store was my favorite business in the entire region. I loved the beautiful antique wooden iceboxes and the silver cash register, which looked like it could have been a prop in an old Western. The fact that they sold everything from camping supplies to horse feed and human food added to the charm. But probably the store's greatest asset was the owner. He appeared to be almost as old as the store and had a long gray beard that might have been home to some small wildlife. He knew everything that was going on within thirty miles of his business, so if you wanted to catch up on the gossip, he could quickly bring you up-to-date. Nearly two years previous, Christie and I had stopped in to grab a snack after being at the Shultzes' on a somewhat less urgent call. Jamie had purchased a goat at an auction, with the idea that it would protect her sheep from predators. It was a large, intimidating goat all right, but it had not been neutered, and no one had filled her in on how badly unneutered male goats smell. For those who have not experienced it, intact male goats produce one of the most disgusting odors in nature, rivaled only by the smell emanating from Bootsy's anal glands. Over my years of practice, I have been exposed to a lot of pretty bad smells, but that of a male goat is the only one that can still induce nausea. Male goats actually urinate on their own heads to exacerbate the fragrance they feel will attract females. With this as their game plan, I'm surprised that any goats have ever reproduced.

Christie and I had been called out by the Shultzes to remedy the problem. After putting it off as long as we could, we donned clothes that were old enough to throw away and then neutered the goat. On our way back from the Shultz place that morning, we got ourselves far enough away from the goat's smell that we could handle a candy bar, and so we'd gone into the store. As we wandered between the shelves, deciding what high-fructose treats to get, we observed the other patrons turning up their noses at us. Evidently, we had just become desensitized enough to the odor that we hadn't realized we had brought it with us. As we paid for our purchases, the proprietor pulled back from the counter.

"Maybe you two'd better clean up before you come in here next time," he said. Christie and I nodded our heads and scurried out.

I avoided going back in for about six months, hoping that would be about the right amount of time for our lack of judgment to have been forgotten. I made a beeline for a granola bar and pulled a can of Coke from the 1940s-vintage cooler with the picture of a teenage girl holding a glass bottle of Coke. Keeping my head down, I made it to the counter just in time to hear the owner say, "Well, you sure smell better this time. Don't stop in here if the Shultzes get another goat you need to fix."

He felt very good now that he knew the whole story, laughing at me, not with me. I forced out a courtesy laugh and went on my way. At least I felt like I could stop back in now that the entire story was out in the open. I had a feeling that we wouldn't be getting any snacks after going to the Shultzes' today.

The road started back up the hill after going through the little town on the river. The truck strained a little as we worked our way up the grade, and at the top we turned into the Shultzes' driveway, only to see them standing in the middle of a tough-looking group of sheep. Christie and I eased ourselves out of our seats, subconsciously putting off what lay ahead of us.

"This is a bad day, Doc," Mr. Shultz said solemnly as he lifted a blue plastic tarp to expose four of his herd who hadn't made it. He shook his head. "I think there may be a couple more that are not long for this world." Jamie had enough tears running down her face that her mascara had moved to nose level.

"We had noticed a group of about six dogs running in a pack a few days ago. I should have let Animal Control know then. Oh, I wish we had."

She was normally a very happy woman, about fifty years old, with short blond hair and a pair of blue overalls she wore when she was working around the sheep.

"Or we could have just shot the darn things," her husband piped up.

Mr. Shultz was known as a gentle, kind man, but today he deserved to be a little upset. He was around the same age as his wife and had a neatly trimmed beard to balance out the lack of hair on his head. He wasn't particularly tall, but he was the kind of guy you wouldn't want to arm-wrestle with. He had a barrel chest, with biceps that barely fit into the sleeves of his shirt.

"And that darn goat didn't help out at all," he continued. "Speaking of that goat, where is he?"

Christie pointed to him silently. There he stood, thirty feet away from the herd, munching hay as if nothing had happened. He didn't even seem to know what all the fuss was about.

"Well, let's see what we're dealing with," I said as I began to walk through the herd.

There were several with minor scrapes and cuts, which could be treated with just antiseptic and injectable antibiotics, but there were others that were not so lucky. One had lost both her ears in the struggle, and her lamb was one of those under the tarp. Another was a lot worse off, with multiple bite wounds over its entire body. I looked up as Christie was staring down at me, a tear coming out of each eye. I nodded and she went over to the truck. We had been together in these situations before and she knew it was time to get the euthanasia solution.

"This one is not going to make it," I told the Shultzes as they acknowledged me with trusting eyes.

The sheep lay quietly on its side, not even flinching when the needle found its way through the wool and into the jugular vein. As tough as these types of situations are, I always feel a tiny bit better when I can put a suffering animal out of its misery.

Fortunately, there seemed to be no other sheep with life-threatening wounds. Christie and Mr. Shultz went about cleaning lacerations and giving antibiotic shots to the less severe cases, while Jamie and I sutured together a few of the larger cuts. Jamie informed me that Mr. Shultz was actually more of a softy than she was and might not be able to handle working on the worst lacerations. Most of the sutured cuts would not hold together well because of the vascular damage that bite injuries do to the skin edges, but at least they would work as a sort of bandage while the wounds started to heal. Our last patient was the one without ears, who had also lost her lamb.

"Do you think this one will make it?" Jamie asked.

I thought about it a few seconds before answering. "Well, she hasn't lost much blood and she really doesn't have to have ears. If the wounds don't get infected, she should be okay."

We cleaned her up and Christie came around with an antibiotic shot for her, which she dramatically objected to.

"I know why she lost her ears," Jamie muttered. "She is the dominant one, always leading the herd. She must have taken the dogs head-on."

It was easy to believe that had been the case, since even though she no longer had ears, the rest of the flock always kept an eye on what she was up to.

Mr. Shultz added, "We even named her Hillary, since she likes to run the show so much."

The First Lady reference did not go over as well with Jamie. She gave him an elbow in the ribs as he chuckled. "You gave her that name," she said. That would be the only humor we would get from the Shultzes that morning, and it was interrupted by the sounds from a distressed little lamb.

On the edge of the embattled flock was a tiny lamb, only a few days old. He was a dirty white color, with a few spots of black interspersed over his torso. He was shivering slightly, trying to keep warm in the March air as he dodged in and out of the ewes and attempted to steal a bit of milk from the ones that were already nursing lambs.

Jamie recognized what was going on. "His mother is one of the ones under the tarp."

The smile she had eked out minutes before as she elbowed her husband was long gone. It was replaced by new tears on her face. She bent over, picking up the hungry little orphan and holding its head against her cheek.

"You poor little guy, what are we going to do with you?"

It appeared that she was asking the lamb, but she was actually asking me. Jamie knew that bottle-fed lambs never thrived as well as those who nursed from their mothers. She had dealt with this before when one of her ewes had triplets and did not have enough milk for all three. Jamie bottle-fed one of the lambs into adulthood, but he never did as well as the others. She now looked expectantly at me, holding the lamb to her chest.

"You had better come up with something, Doc. Otherwise, she is going to be up every hour for weeks bottle-feeding this guy," Mr. Shultz said as he put his arm around his wife's shoulders, giving her a supportive hug. "In reality, she will talk me into doing it part of the time, so neither of us will get any sleep."

Well, we had a mother without a baby and a baby without a mother. I brought up the obvious. "I doubt that Hillary is going to voluntarily take on a lamb that isn't hers. She just doesn't appear to have the personality for it."

Occasionally, what I learned in veterinary school was not as valuable as what I picked up from people along the way. My dad had shown me as a boy how to trick obstinate ewes into taking on babies that were not theirs. It was an old trick, but still a good one. The plan was simply to put Vicks in the nostrils of the ewe so that she could not distinguish the smell of a lamb that was not her biological one. Animals have such a developed sense of smell that they can detect their offspring just by their individual odor. When the ewe's sense of smell is blocked by the Vicks, she is more apt to accept a lamb that is not hers. What could it hurt? The lamb needed a mother.

"There may be a way we could help to encourage this relationship," I offered, and I went on to explain the plan.

The couple listened intently but looked uncertain. "I hope that you didn't have to go through years of veterinary school to figure that one out, Doc!" Mr. Shultz got a little kick out of this as he said it. He continued: "How are we going to keep her still for all of this?"

"Well, we're going to have to rig a gate to swing around so that we can pin her against the fence for now. The gate will have to have big-enough openings between the boards so the lamb can get its head in to nurse." A slight tilt of the head, followed by a thoughtful nod, indicated his approval. "Now, I don't usually carry Vicks on the truck, so—"

Jamie quickly interrupted. "I've got some in the medicine cabinet. I'll grab it."

Mr. Shultz got started putting together the gate system to pin Hillary in while Jamie went for the Vicks.

Christie, who had kept fairly quiet during the whole ordeal, now finally spoke up. "Do you actually think this is going to work?"

"You have a better idea?" I replied. After thinking a second, I apologized. "I'm sorry. That didn't come out the way I'd planned. I don't know if it will work, but it might. After all that the Shultzes have been through today, I just want something to work out for them."

"I know," said Christie. "I want that, too."

Jamie returned with the Vicks and Mr. Shultz got the gate rear-ranged. It took the four of us to capture Hillary once she realized she was the one we wanted. We practically had to carry her into the make-shift holding cage. Then, to add to her frustration, I covered her nostrils with Vicks. It seemed like a lot to put an animal through that had just lost its ears, but the orphan lamb was still beside us, begging for food.

"I think we are as ready as we are going to be," Mr. Shultz announced.

He stood proudly beside the captured sheep with no ears, who was sneezing Vicks out of her nose. Jamie scooted the little guy up to the gate and he stuck his head through. His woolly tail whirled around like a helicopter blade, the way a lamb's tail does when the animal is taking in milk. The lamb nursed until his previously gaunt flanks ballooned out on both sides. He was so tired from nursing that he walked over to a pile of uneaten hay, collapsed, and fell immediately asleep. Even Hillary's periodic kicking hadn't hindered his gorging. I rubbed his head and he didn't budge. He had been putting off sleep in hope of a meal, and Hillary had reluctantly provided one.

"I guess we are going to be repeating this scene for a while," said Mr. Shultz. "I am seeing some sleep deprivation in my future."

"But you wouldn't have it any other way, would you, honey?" Jamie gave him a squeeze as she said it.

"I'll do whatever we need to do to save this poor little guy," he replied, scratching the sleeping youngster under the chin.

Jamie gave her husband a quick kiss. "That's why I love him."

"Hopefully, Hillary will start to accept him as her own before long and you won't have to keep going through this procedure," I said in an effort to encourage them, but in reality I knew that some ewes never accept orphan lambs. "We'll be back tomorrow to re-treat the injured ones and check up on Hillary's new lamb." Christie and I cleaned up our mess and went on our way.

Inside the truck, Christie asked the question that I knew she would. "Do you really think that Hillary is going to accept that lamb?" Sometimes Christie was not the most positive person.

"I sure hope that she does; otherwise, it is going to be a long haul for the Shultzes." I felt the same way as she did, but I was trying to stay as positive as I could. "Let's get a treat. We deserve one today," I told Christie as I swung the truck into the general store's parking lot.

As I opened the squeaky old screen door, the owner squinted at us from the back of the store. I knew what he was thinking. "Don't worry, just blood and Vicks on us today," I said.

He grinned slightly before responding. "Are any of the Shultz flock going to make it? Word is, they took a pretty big hit."

"We haven't lost too many, but we'll be back tomorrow to check on them again," I said as I paid for our granola bars.

He gave me an approving nod. "Take care of those critters. The Shultzes are good people." Christie promised we would and we got ourselves back on the road.

The next day, Christie and I headed back to the Shultz place first thing in the morning. Jamie and her husband already had Hillary restrained and the lamb was gorging himself again.

"She has been getting less patient with the lamb every time we force her into letting him eat. We went through this three times last night, and after the last time, she tried to attack him when we let her go. We had to take him back to the house with us for his safety," Mr. Shultz said with a yawn.

I didn't need to ask if they were still using the Vicks on Hillary. The whole place had that medicine smell, especially Mr. Shultz.

Christie and I went about our duties, re-treating the wounds from the day before. The last sheep we rechecked was Hillary. What was left of her ears looked much better, but her attitude was not good. She seemed to know that I might be responsible for her struggle with the new lamb, and she wiped her Vicks-covered nose all over me. No stopping for a granola bar today. We would have been kicked out of the store for sure.

"We'll come back one more time in the morning, and after that, you guys should be able to take it from there," I informed Jamie.

"Oh, thanks again for coming, but I don't think that Hillary is going to take on that poor little lamb." She was very concerned. "I'm afraid that she is really going to hurt him."

I agreed with her. "Let's give them twenty-four hours longer and then we may have to start bottle-feeding." Jamie agreed, and we headed off to our next stop. The third morning we trekked back to the Shultzes', Christie had brought along a small bottle, a rubber nipple, and a milk substitute. I hadn't fought her, giving in to the inevitable fact that Hillary was not going to take on the hungry little orphan. When we pulled in, no one was to be found but sheep munching hay. Jamie and Mr. Shultz had obviously given up grafting the pair and were just catching up on sleep. We spotted Hillary in the group, but no lamb. The dreaded tarp lay off to the side and Christie walked cautiously toward it. She slowly bent down, lifted a corner, and peaked underneath.

"Nothing here!" she yelled with great relief.

Hillary seemed even more agitated than she had the day before, pacing around the corral and stomping her foot. Now our curiosity was getting the better of us, and we walked toward the house to find out what was up. Just before we got to the door, it flew open and out came the lamb at a dead run, headed for the rest of the sheep, followed by Jamie and Mr. Shultz. Even more surprising was that Hillary was calling to the little guy. He ran right up to her and began nursing madly. She didn't move a stitch, only nosing him to encourage the eating. Jamie, seeing the bewildered looks on our faces, went on to explain. "We were close to giving up last evening, but then the neighbors came over to see how our flock was doing and they happened to bring their Sheltie with them. It tried to play with the orphan lamb, and Hillary had a fit. She ran right over, claiming the lamb for her own." Jamie beamed with relief. "They have been mother and son ever since. She even lets him nurse with no restraint." She paused for a few seconds. "We do have another problem, though. They need you to stop over and take a look at the Sheltie. Hillary worked him over pretty good."

Llama Mayhem

Mr. Habben greeted me in the driveway, wearing a clear plastic face shield and a bright yellow poncho-style raincoat. He waved his right hand and gave me a wide, welcoming smile full of bright teeth. He was a tall, slender man, about thirty-five, with lots of coal black hair jutting out around the straps on his head that held the face mask in place. I had not met Mr. Habben before, and he appeared a little psychotic standing there in his costume. It wasn't raining; in fact, it was a beautiful sunny day in the Rockies. So what was up with the face mask? As it turned out, this outfit had a specific purpose.

For those not well acquainted with llamas: they are a member of the camel family and have a couple similarities. Their necks are extremely long, almost snakelike. The soles of their feet are relatively soft and well padded for walking on less than stable surfaces. These specialized hooves have made them very popular in the Rocky Mountain area as pack animals, because they cause minimal damage to the fragile alpine terrain. Llamas are significantly smaller than camels and come from the Peruvian Andes instead of from the desert. Like camels, they have multiple stomachs designed to digest food thoroughly (cows and deer do also). Animals with multiple stomach chambers are sometimes called "ruminates" because they actually regurgitate what they have eaten back into their mouths so that they can chew it again. This process helps to maximize the amount of nutrition they get out of each bite.

Unfortunately for us, llamas and camels share one less than favorable trait. They regurgitate and spit at those they consider aggressors, something you will never see a cow or deer do.

I have never concentrated on llama work, even though there are large numbers of them in Colorado. In fact, I have tried to avoid them. It's not that I don't like them; it's just that I've never really felt qualified to treat them. Due to my lack of knowledge in llama medicine, I usually referred them to another veterinarian in the area, someone who really had a handle on their diseases and ailments.

This particular morning, Lorraine had caught me at the door. "We got a call from one of Dr. Davis's llama clients. He said his llamas needed a manicure and that Dr. Davis said to call you."

"Well, try to work them in today if you can," I responded somewhat reluctantly. I wanted to say, Wait a couple hours to call back and maybe they will have called someone else, but I didn't.

Dr. Davis usually seemed to appreciate my referrals, yet once in a while I felt like she wanted to get back at me a little. As a result, I would find myself on a llama call that she had sent my way for a reason. This stop at Mr. Habben's was one of those times.

"So you're the one who drew the short straw." Mr. Habben smiled as he looked me up and down. "You ought to do, but I hope you are quick."

"Just how quick will I need to be?" I asked, curious. "You did just want me to trim their feet today?"

Mr. Habben chuckled from behind his face mask and then took off toward the two llamas in the pasture, looking like a badly dressed superhero. I grabbed the steel hoof trimmers out of the truck, then trotted to catch up with Mr. Habben.

The llamas had strategically placed themselves at the farthest end of the property. They were grazing contently as Mr. Habben and I approached. Once we got within about one hundred yards of them, they started to get a little nervous. They began spending more time keeping an eye on us than on eating. When we closed in at fifty yards, Mr. Habben stopped me to explain his plan of attack.

"We need to move them toward the shed, then get them inside to corner them." He pointed to a three-sided building in the middle of the pasture. It appeared to be in fairly good condition, and the plan seemed reasonable overall.

Most serious llama owners have the animals trained to walk into a little fenced area, where they then allow themselves to be tied to a post with a llama halter. In this way, they could be worked on with relative ease and safety. I decided to bring up this possibility with Mr. Habben.

"Are they trained to be tied once we get them in the shed?"

He wrinkled his face, like he had no idea what I was talking about. "Oh, no. These guys came with the place when we bought it. The previous owners couldn't catch them when they moved, so they just left them behind."

This was not the first time I had encountered hoofed animals left behind when the owners moved, and the passed-along beasts always seemed to have a less than favorable attitude.

I had one client who had inherited two virtually wild horses when he purchased his dream mountain property. They were beautiful golden-colored animals with flaxen manes and tails, but they lost some of their appeal when the owner tried to catch them. They ran him right out of the field. After two months of work with a trainer, they allowed themselves to be caught. The owner then decided that it was time for the pair to be vaccinated and dewormed, so he called the office and set up an appointment. When I walked into the pasture, they ran toward me, jumped the creek between us, and backed up to kick at me as if I were some kind of predator. One of them nailed me in the hip before I made the fence. The owner explained that kicking newcomers was the horses' way of saying hi, but somehow I didn't really see it.

These llamas would not be exceptions to this pattern.

By flapping our arms and yelling a little, we began moving the llamas toward the awaiting shed. "The smaller one is Timmy and the larger one is Tommy," Mr. Habben informed me. "Timmy is pretty easy and won't give us much trouble, but Tommy will be a different story."

As the llamas closed in on their potential confines, Tommy began to get a little worried. He threw his long neck into the air and cocked his head into an on-guard position. He watched our every movement, ears pointed forward so as not to miss a sound. Reluctantly, he moved toward the shed. Meanwhile, Timmy walked quietly in the proper direction, stopping only to grab a few bites of grass along the way. The pair finally moved into the open side of the shed, while Mr. Habben and I closed in. We made our move to swing the large metal gate closed and thereby capture them inside the building. Tommy decided that this was not such a good idea. We were within a few inches of getting the gate shut when Tommy reared his head and flattened his ears back against his neck, resembling a cobra positioned to strike. This aggressive behavior is not uncommon in unneutered male llamas, and it always freaks me out just a little. Tommy then began to

move his jaw back and forth, as if he had a large piece of chewing gum stuck to the roof of his mouth. He looked me right in the eye from the distance of only a few yards, snapped his head forward, and spat right on my cheek. The direct shot distracted me just long enough that I let go of the gate, and Tommy took the chance to push through the opening. Mr. Habben, although upset that Tommy had gotten away, couldn't hold back his glee at seeing an inexperienced llama vet be initiated by a direct hit.

"Oh, he got you good." Mr. Habben laughed. "Rookie mistake."

He was so amused at me standing there with spit on my face

that I thought he would never get back to the task at hand. Even with Tommy's bad behavior, we had still managed to capture one llama.

Timmy stood in the building, completely content and seemingly oblivious of Tommy's antics. He even seemed to know that it was time to give in and let us do what we needed to do. To my amazement, Timmy let me pick up his left front foot and trim the hoof back to where it should be. In ten minutes, I had trimmed all four feet, and then Mr. Habben let him go back into the pasture. Now it was time to give Tommy another try.

We regrouped and moved Tommy back toward the shed again. He hadn't wandered far, sticking close to his buddy. As we got him close to the shed, he started to dance around and began forming another spitball in his mouth. Before we could get him into the gated area, he ran straight up to me and stuck his face into mine, threatening me with another spit wad. Mr. Habben saw what was about to happen and ran toward Tommy, trying to distract him from me.

"Shoo, get away, you big bugger!" Mr. Habben yelled. Tommy turned toward him, wiggled his lips, and fired the spit at Mr. Habben.

It landed directly on the face mask, and I could see a knowing smile creep across his face behind the mask, a smile of pride at being smart enough to have worn the proper equipment for the job. Tommy was still more than a little agitated, but Mr. Habben got him headed for the shed and, with the speed of a gazelle, got the gate closed behind him. Tommy was not pleased and shot another spit wad, which was blocked by the yellow poncho. Both Mr. Habben and I climbed over the gate at the same time, cornering Tommy in the shed. This gave Tommy the illusion that it was time to give in.

We caught our breath for a few minutes and laughed about being spat on by an upset llama. In actuality, we were procrastinating. Both of us knew that trimming Tommy's feet was going to be far from simple and might even be life-threatening.

Eventually, I had to face the music, and I went to pick up the first foot. Tommy wasn't going to let me get away that easy. He was experienced, having won this battle with delusional veterinarians before. He immediately collapsed onto his stomach, tucking all four legs under him. They just disappeared into his excessive hair and underbelly. "I knew this wasn't going to be pretty." Mr. Habben snickered. "I hope you have a better plan than that." He came forward and attempted to help me get Tommy back onto his feet, but trying to lift a determined 350-pound llama is an impossible task. Even the two of us couldn't lift him an inch. "All I can think to do is give him some sedation to take the edge off," I announced.

"Oh no," he responded. "Tried that once before, and it just makes it even harder to get him off his legs." I was learning that everything we were doing had been attempted multiple times before. Now Mr. Habben just stood there in his spit-repulsion gear waiting for my next move. All I could come up with was to roll Tommy over somehow and get his legs out from under him.

With Mr. Habben's help, I attempted to push Tommy over on his side. If the big fur ball could have laughed at us, he would have.

Mr. Habben stared at Tommy, then spoke up. "When I played football, we would put our shoulders into the blocking dummy to move it down the field. I wonder if we could lean into Tommy with our shoulders and shove him over."

It sounded like as good a plan as any, so we each bent down, buried one shoulder into Tommy's oily long hair, and shoved. Grunting and sweating, we barely got him to move at all off center. There was no way that we would get him onto his side, but it was just enough for me to pull one rear leg out from underneath him. It was also just enough for him to reach up and kick me in the ankle with the same foot—not just a little swat, but a loud, cracking slap. It hurt enough to make me see stars, but I couldn't let Mr. Habben see how much pain I was in. He was getting way too much entertainment out of the whole situation as it was.

"That isn't the first time he has nailed a vet." He giggled. "He's gotten me several times, too."

To add insult to injury, Tommy had also pulled the leg back under him, so we would have to start the whole procedure over. "This time, could you jump in and grab hold of the leg also?" I asked Mr. Habben. He nodded sheepishly and we repeated the scenario.

This round, when I got the leg out, Mr. Habben jumped in and helped. With his assistance, I was able to get the foot trimmed without more llama-induced pain, and Tommy didn't get the leg back under him until we released it. We reenacted the old football game plan until all four feet were trimmed, by which time we were dosed in sweat and oily llama residue. Exhausted, we both stood bent over beside the freshly pedicured llama. Hands on our knees, we waited for strength to flow back into our bodies. Mr. Habben, who had recuperated faster than I had, disappeared for a few moments. He soon returned with a can of Coke for each of us.

"You deserve it," he barked as he shoved the cold can into my clammy hand. "You're the first vet to accomplish this mission since I've owned them."

The soda hit the back of my throat, giving me both liquid and much-needed sugar at the same time.

I thanked Mr. Habben for the drink, grabbed my hoof trimmers, and started to walk to the truck. I didn't see Mr. Habben open the gate and let Tommy run free into the pasture. I didn't hear the soft steps of llama feet in the grass, running up behind me. But I did feel the wet llama spit hit my back and soak through my shirt. I turned around, to find Tommy staring me in the face. He was letting me know that I had not completely won and that next time wasn't going to be as easy. Then he turned and trotted off to rejoin Timmy. Oh how I hoped that there wouldn't be a next time.

Not Thinking

Horses had been a big part of my life ever since I could remember. When I turned five, my grandfather bought me a pony. Now, most people would say what a lucky little boy to be given a pony at such a young age, but that is only because they don't know the rest of the story.

This wasn't the kind of pony that children imagine riding across open fields on and jumping over fences with. Oh yes, there was a lot of running involved, but it wasn't my decision. Tina was a black one-year-old Shetland pony with a flowing black mane and tail. Shetlands are a small, cute breed, but they are known to be very mischievous, and Tina more than lived up to the breed's reputation. I think my grandfather probably paid about fifty dollars for her at the time, and I'm sure that my parents accrued many times that in medicals bills from my subsequent injuries.

When Tina turned two years old, my dad decided she was old enough to ride, yet the only one small enough to sit on her back was me. So my dad bought a tiny saddle and placed me on her back, then led her around the yard. Tina would perform so perfectly that my dad would eventually tell me to grasp the reins tightly; then he'd unhook the lead rope and set off to work on another project. The minute he was out of sight, Tina would gather her little legs, lower her petite head, and take off at a dead run, bucking at the same time. Sometimes I would come off early in the game, but other times I would be filled with determination, holding on until the saddle, with me still in it, slipped underneath her.

During the late sixties in rural Iowa, wearing a protective helmet to ride a horse was unheard of. The result was that my head bounced off the ground like a basketball as Tina dashed across the open fields. Once she unloaded me, the fun was over for her, so she would just stop and graze contentedly, even with the saddle still hanging under her. This scenario played out for a few years. I was determined that she would give in any day, but Tina knew that wasn't going to happen. Eventually, it was my father who gave up and bought me a well-trained pony that I could ride. Tina got what she wanted—a life of grazing, uninterrupted by humans. Given this early experience, one would assume that I would never have attempted to train a horse to ride again, but time heals most wounds and makes us forget.

Tami Mercer owned a barnful of huge show horses bred for jumping. She herself was a petite woman, which made her horses seem even larger than they really were. Since she had several horses and took meticulous care of them, I ended up at her barn on a fairly regular basis. I went to the farm one day to treat a horse that was lame. The horse's right front leg been getting progressively worse over the last forty-eight hours.

"When it comes to equine lameness, always check the foot first; otherwise, you will miss the obvious!" I remember my instructor yelling this at us while standing at the front of the lecture hall. To his credit, he could not have been more correct, and I heard his voice in my head as I picked up the lame leg to check the hoof.

Putting the animal's leg between my knees, I held it there while I used a tool called a "hoof tester" to look for a sensitive spot on the bottom of the foot. This tool looks sort of like a large pair of pliers, with a modified pinching area for finding the spot that the horse reacts to. After squeezing a few different spots, I hit the one that caused the horse to pull his foot away.

"That must be it. Do you think it's an abscess?" Tami had been around horses long enough to have a pretty good knowledge of the most common lameness problems.

"We're about to find out," I replied as I traded the hoof tester for a hoof knife. This little tool is not much bigger than the blade of a pocketknife and has a wooden handle and a sharp hook on the end for digging out infections in the hoof. Hoof abscesses have always been my favorite kind of lameness to treat. Once you find the source of the problem and drain out the infection, the animal usually begins to improve almost immediately. Using the hook at the end of the blade, I scraped away at the sore spot until dark pus rolled out of the resulting hole.

"Yes, I'm so glad it's not something worse. I should be able to ride him again soon, shouldn't I?" she asked hopefully.

"I think so. You will have to change the wrap daily and we'll get him started on some antibiotics." I always hedged my answers a little, just in case the infection went deeper than it appeared.

Tami held the leg up while I flushed the abscess with iodine and wrapped it. I handed her some antibiotic powder to put on the open sore over the next week and grabbed a receipt out of the cab to start writing up the bill. Tami sometimes had trouble paying her bills, so I usually presented her with one right away to avoid embarrassing collection calls in the future. She had usually been really good about paying me on the spot when I handed her the bill, but on this day she seemed a little more nervous than usual as I finished my calculations.

When I handed the bill to her, she stared at it for a minute. Then she rubbed her chin and said, "I want to show you something. Come with me."

It was obvious that she was going to have trouble coming up with the money for this one. What in the heck is she going to show me? I wondered The chances of getting paid right away weren't looking so good.

We headed for the back portion of the barn, an area where I had not been before. The stalls got darker the farther back we got, and most of them were empty. She stopped in front of the last stall, pulling down the huge halter that was hooked on the door and wiggling the latch to get it open. Whatever was inside blew a frightening burst of air through its nostrils to let us know it wasn't happy to be disturbed.

"Easy, big guy," Tami whispered before she disappeared into the murky stall.

I heard the stomping of an unhappy foot on the earthen floor; then out through the doorway burst what at the time seemed like the largest equine I had ever seen. He was dragging Tami behind him like a fish attached to a whale.

"Slow down, Wyoming. Now stop it!"

Tami got some traction in the alleyway between the stalls, just enough to convince the beast to run in circles around her instead of taking a straight shot to the open end of the barn. He tore around with his head down and his ears laid back while blowing up dirt with his huge nostrils. Tami appeared satisfied with this, acting as if circling was the best behavior she expected from him. Apparently, getting him to stand still was not an option with this medieval-looking equine. It didn't take much imagination to picture him carrying a knight in full armor.

"My ex-husband and I adopted him and his mother off the plains of Wyoming when he was just a foal. His mother was a wild mare, and his father was a draft horse that belonged to one of the local ranchers. The Bureau of Land Management rounded them up and put them up for adoption. I always thought I would break him to ride, but after the divorce, I just never got to it, and that was nine years ago." She continued to explain. "He is such a gentle creature, I'm sure it would take nothing to train him, and he would make a wonderful riding horse."

That was not actually what I was thinking as I watched him tear madly around Tami. In my naïveté, I did not realize the reason for this demonstration, but I was about to find out.

"How much would you give me for him?" she blurted out while looking straight at me.

A little shocked, I didn't really know what to say. The fact that she didn't budge or even look away told me that she was dead serious. An older, more savvy veterinarian would have walked away from this scene with an appropriate "No" and moved on with his life, but back then I was still young enough to lack judgment. Testosterone often seems to block the decision-making part of young men's brains, resulting in completely illogical moves. In my mind, I began to look at it as a challenge, and as I answered her question, I couldn't believe my own ears.

"I'll give you a hundred bucks off today's bill," I announced.

I think a part of me hoped that this would not be nearly enough, but Tami responded with lightning speed. "I'll take it, and I will deliver him."

This was not a good sign. She didn't even try to dicker. What was

I going to do with this crazy horse? I was a little dazed as I rewrote the bill, a hundred dollars less than the original.

Tami seemed elated. "I'll bring him by on Saturday afternoon. See you then!" She was way too cheerful.

On the way home, I kept going over my spontaneous decision. What was I going to tell my wife, Marion, and what would she think? When I got home, Marion was not back from work yet, so I began fixing up the old corral fence that the previous owner had used to contain her horse. It wasn't the best, but with some new wire and posts, it could be brought back to life.

When Marion arrived home, she seemed a little surprised at my news and admitted she might have made a different decision, yet she agreed that it might be kind of fun.

The following Friday, Tami called to let me know that she would be bringing the big horse by on Saturday. She seemed overly enthusiastic about the drop-off, but it was too late to back out. If I changed my mind now, I would lose her as a client for sure. On Saturday morning about nine o'clock, I heard the whinny of an upset horse coming down the road in front of our house. I stepped out of the front door just as Tami's truck and trailer pulled into the driveway.

"Looks like the right place," Tami yelled. "I hope you're ready for him." She whipped back to the rear of the trailer with a lead rope that she had grabbed from the bed of the pickup.

Wyoming sensed that she was about to let him out, and he began to slam his foot against the trailer floor, demanding his immediate release. Tami slid open the latch on the back doors and they flew open as the horse leaped from his confines prematurely. Tami turned her left shoulder into the flinging door in anticipation of the impact, but it still knocked her off her feet. The big brown horse hit the end of the lead rope that Tami had managed to hold on to, and he turned back toward her. Head bowed and muscles tense, he let out a defiant snort to establish his displeasure. At this point, I was almost hoping that he would just keep running. What the heck was I going to do with him?

Tami brushed herself off and began walking toward our barn as if this was just normal behavior for any horse.

"Where do you want him?" she asked while spitting out small bits of gravel she had nearly ingested while on the ground.

"Over there in the round pen, I guess," I said, pointing to the fence I had just repaired, but now I wondered if it would be enough.

Tami walked ahead of me and swung open the metal gate at one end of the pen. Wyoming shoved past her, bolting into his new surroundings. Tami popped open the steel snap at the end of the lead rope and the big horse threw his head in the air, then trotted around his new home, sniffing the ground for the scent of every horse that had come before him. Tami slammed the gate shut before Wyoming could decide to leave, letting out a sigh, which she tried to hide from me.

"Congratulations. He's all yours," she proclaimed with a smile as she handed me the lead rope. It was as if she'd passed me a baton that she didn't want back.

As I looked down at the rope hanging from my hand, I managed to get out a weak "Thank you."

"Well, I had better get going. I've got a new boarder coming in this afternoon and I've got to clean out Wyoming's old stall for him." Now I was starting to really catch on. She scampered up into her truck and was gone.

Fortunately, Marion had missed out on the delivery. She came out of the house just as Tami drove off. Right when she got outside, Wyoming let out series of snorts, then tore around his corral with the demeanor of a wild animal.

"Are you sure that this is a good idea? He doesn't look too happy to be here." Her forehead wrinkled as she watched the crazed equine stomp his front foot in disapproval of his new situation.

"I'm afraid he's ours now," I replied.

I had developed a case of buyer's remorse, to say the least, but unlike most regrettable purchases, this one might actually kill me.

I ran some water through a hose from the house into a plastic trough that was in the corral and grabbed a flake of hay from the barn. Wyoming's huge head reached over the fence as I tried to toss the hay in, and he snatched it before I could get it out of my hands, his front teeth snapping together only an inch from my fingers. It was as if I were feeding a prehistoric animal who might bite my fingers off or sprout wings and come flying over the fence. I knew I had to get over this irrational fear, or I would never be able to be around this horse, let alone be able to train him to ride.

The next morning before I left for work, I walked down to feed and water Wyoming again, and this time he charged the fence, ears laid back and teeth flashing.

"Easy, buddy. Haven't you ever heard not to bite the hand that feeds you?" I muttered, thinking that talking to him might soothe him.

Instead, it just made him angrier. He threw his head in the air and flared his nostrils at me, as if trying to provoke a fight.

After tossing his hay in from a safe distance, I arched water from a hose into his bucket, never getting closer than five feet to the wooden rails that kept him at bay. I had dealt with a lot of tough horses in my practice, but Wyoming seemed to take the cake.

That evening, Marion watched as the same scene unfolded. "I think we had better rename him. I don't believe that Wyoming is descriptive enough."

"I agree. What do you have in mind?" Being killed by an animal named Wyoming wouldn't be that impressive. "How about Widow Maker?" I suggested. That was the kind of name that would be used in a rodeo and would look good on a tombstone.

"How about Ivan? Ivan the Terrible?" she responded.

That did seem to fit, and so Ivan it was from that day on.

I yelled to him, "So what do you think about that, Ivan?" He stomped and pawed at the dirt, which I took for a yes.

Over the next month, I kept trying to work with the beast every chance I got. By week two, he began to let me in the pen with him, and as a reward I started giving him carrots. He acted as if he had never had them before, smelling them first to be sure I was not attempting to poison him, or, worse yet, tranquilize him. By using the carrots, I was able to bribe him to let me touch his head and eventually even rub his neck.

"Hey, big guy, that's pretty good stuff. Maybe I'm not the equine Antichrist after all." He looked at me out of the corner of his eye, as if to say, I haven't totally ruled that out, but it is looking less likely.

The days went by, and Ivan progressed to accepting a halter and even working at the end of a longe line. He would trot around me at the end of the long nylon strap, occasionally taking a swipe at me with a back leg, just to see if I was still paying attention.

We worked up to him wearing a saddle during our training sessions. As expected, this didn't go over well at first and required a lot of carrots. He gave in eventually, which led up to the step that I had been dreading the most: saddle with rider in it.

The day had arrived. It could not be avoided any longer. I convinced Marion to hold the lead rope and walk Ivan around inside his corral once I got mounted. I donned an old bicycle helmet just in case things didn't go my way.

"Are you sure you want to do this? No one will think less of you if you don't. We can hire a trainer, you know." Women don't realize that these are the absolute last words they should ever use to convince a man not to do something.

When we hear "No one will think less of you," we receive a rush of testosterone that overcomes any rational fear, causing us to proceed with whatever idiotic feat we should not be doing. So with that, I placed my left foot in the stirrup, threw myself into the saddle, and faced death head-on.

Ivan flinched a bit when my butt hit the saddle and he skirted off to the side. His muscles tensed in preparation to spring. My right hand grasped the saddle horn with a strength that I didn't know I had, giving new meaning to the term *white knuckling.*

"Well, are you ready to start moving?" Marion asked.

Nodding cautiously, I took my first steps with Ivan. He was great! All the groundwork had made a real difference. It was as if he had been waiting to be ridden his whole life. As good as he was, it took me several repeat performances to release my death hold on the saddle horn.

One afternoon, I got home from work a little early and decided it was time to move to the next level with Ivan. Marion was not home yet, so my foolishness could not be observed. Getting the tack on and mounting up went without a glitch. A touch in Ivan's side with my boot gave him the signal that it was time to move forward. The next thing I knew, his head was so high that his ears were in my face. He realized Marion was not in front of him. His security blanket was gone, and he wasn't happy about it. Just as quickly as his head had come up, it then dropped between his legs. In a fraction of a second, his rear legs gathered and he tossed me into the air. My posterior reconnected with the saddle on the way down, but I had lost my balance. Now it was only a matter of time. His front end bounced into the air and my shoulders connected with the hard Colorado ground.

Air, I needed air, but the fall had knocked it out of me and I couldn't seem to get it back. My lungs heaved in an attempt to refill as I knelt on all fours, unaware that Ivan was ripping around his corral, careful not to crush me as he ran. I didn't even notice the scrapes and bruises I had gotten during my flight from the ejection seat and my hard landing.

Just as I began to think that I might live, Marion's voice pierced my fog. "Are you okay? Did you break anything?" Her hand was on my shoulder as she knelt beside me. She had gotten home just in time to see me on the ground.

By this time, I was beginning to feel a bit embarrassed by my weakened state and how I had gotten there, but when I stood upright, the pain hit. The slightest turn of my neck or back nearly sent me back to the ground.

"I think we should probably go to the hospital just to get me checked out, even though I'm sure it's nothing," I said meekly. Marion rolled her eyes in response and helped me get to her car.

Many X-rays later it was determined in the emergency room that I had cracked portions of three vertebrae. The radiologist advised me to take off the next six weeks and rest, but he did not understand veterinary practice. The next day, I was back at work, but even removing porcupine quills from a dog nearly put me on my knees.

At home, Ivan watched me from his confines as if he felt bad. He would even whinny at me occasionally, seeming to want attention. Over the next several weeks, my back healed and I was able to turn my body without passing out. As I improved, I was able to at least limp down to rub his nose and give him the occasional carrot. Before long, it was time to give Ivan another try. We started from the ground up again, with Marion leading me; then one day, I tried it on my own, although Marion was right there. The big guy and I even went on a few short trail rides together, but I knew I didn't have the skill to train him to his full capability.

A few weeks later, I was vaccinating some horses at a local stable when the resident trainer approached me. I had known Tiffany for a few years now and she was as good with a horse as they come. She strode up in her tight riding pants, English boots, and sleeveless shirt. She was about thirty, tall, and very thin. Her hair was extra blond from her time in the sun and her face was overly tanned. She was a very striking figure as she stood silhouetted in the open door of the barn, watching me examine a horse.

"I've heard that you have a big horse you are working with. I am looking for a jumper after mine came up lame." She paused before asking, "Do you think you would be interested in me working with him so I could take him to some shows? I can't afford a new horse right now."

At first, I thought Marion had put her up to this, but what if she had? Tiffany was a lot more qualified to train a horse like Ivan than I was. Besides, I needed to be able to walk and talk if I was to keep practicing.

"Sure, you can give him a try. Just be careful. He's quite a character and has put me in the hospital once already." I wanted to be sure she knew what she was getting into.

"Great!" she exclaimed, practically jumping for joy. "I'll be over to get him next week."

I brought it up with Marion when I got home and she denied having had anything to do with it. There was no reason to doubt her, yet she did seem a little too happy that someone else would be taking over the responsibility for Ivan's schooling. One trip to the emergency room was enough for her.

Having left a message with Tiffany to call me when she was ready to pick him up, I waited for her call. She would no doubt need some help just getting him from the corral to the driveway, and maybe even some sedative to get him into the trailer. It was easy to imagine him yanking against the lead rope, dragging Tiffany around the yard when she attempted to load him.

On Wednesday evening, I stepped out of the truck in disbelief. There was no call from the corral. Ivan and his massive red halter were gone. Since horse thieves don't steal horses like Ivan, for fear of life and limb, I had to assume that Tiffany had somehow gotten him out and loaded him up. Relieved not to find any blood in the area where she would have parked the trailer, I couldn't resist driving over to her stable to see how things were going.

Veering off the pavement and passing Tiffany's still-intact but empty trailer, I continued past the well-kept barns. At the end of the last building were the white-painted boards that circled the riding arena, or soon to be rodeo arena if Ivan didn't behave. I could just make out a rider and horse at the far end of the arena. They began loping through the sandy footing toward me. It couldn't be, but it was. Tiffany was already riding Ivan, and the two of them looked just great.

"Bet you didn't expect to see this!" she yelled as she pulled him to a stop in front of me.

"I didn't think you would be able to get him here by yourself, let alone be able to ride him right away." I'm sure I looked more than a little astonished.

Evidently, Tiffany had immediately gained Ivan's trust, and vice versa. The two of them seemed to be made for each other. Within a matter of months, the pair were going to shows and winning ribbons. Marion and I attended a couple, in one of which Ivan outperformed many well-bred, expensive horses.

"Is that your horse?" people would ask when we cheered for him and Tiffany. "What is his lineage?"

I never had the heart to tell them the truth, knowing they had most likely spent thousands on their animals. I did tell one lady that he was a "Wyoming warmblood," a term that was met with a rather baffled reaction.

The day that I'd anticipated eventually came. I was out at Tiffany's stable to write a health certificate on Ivan for an out-of-state show. Tiffany approached me and said, "I would like to have my name under 'Owner' on this paperwork next time." She looked me right in the eyes, not even blinking as she waited for an answer.

Losing the stare-down, I broke into a smile. "Well, I'm sure that could be arranged."

I would miss Ivan, but I knew this was the right spot for him. Tiffany loved him, and I figured that he must love her, too, or he would have let her know different by now. I sold him to her for a very reasonable price, a little more than the original trade, but not a lot.

Tiffany was elated. She went on showing Ivan and doing very well. I was glad the big horse was in good hands and also a little bit glad that I wouldn't feel pressure to ride him again. I would always have to laugh when I thought how upset the competitors must have been when they found out they were outdone by a hundred-dollar horse.

Baby-Sitter

I swung open the now-familiar gate to the Hansberger ranch and drew in the smell of summer sage in South Park. I was welcomed once again by the committee of goldens. They didn't bark at me as much as they used to; just a couple little yips, followed by big slob-bering smiles and lots of tail wagging. I was a familiar sight now, not worth wasting a lot of energy on.

I had by now been to the ranch more times than I could count. I had been there to treat horses and cattle, but this time it was a golden retriever issue. The greeting party was one short today.

Mrs. Hansberger had called about ten that morning. "Tara is hav-ing puppies as we speak. They're coming kind of slow. Do you think you could come out this afternoon and check on her?"

Birthing puppies in South Park was not something that was going to fit neatly into my schedule on a summer day, but I conceded.

"I'll see if we can move things around a little bit. I'll plan on see-ing you early this afternoon."

Lorraine sighed while rolling her eyes. She had overheard the conversation and knew this translated to her calling clients to move the appointments around.

"You do it to me every time," she said, shaking her head as she went over to the phone.

I did often have to make adjustments in the daily schedule, but it was the nature of the beast. One has to prioritize when it comes to the more life-threatening calls.

Holly yelled from the doorway, "Come on in. They're in the living room."

I followed Holly through the kitchen and on into the main room. In the center was a large wooden box full of squealing little blond puppies. Mrs. Hansberger was kneeling over them. Tara lay in the middle on her right side; she was restless and not paying much attention to the pups. Meanwhile, the puppies' father was outside chasing rabbits and playing with the other dogs. Typical male.

"The puppies are whining a lot. I don't think they are getting much to eat yet. Do you think there is something wrong with Tara?" Mrs. Hansberger asked.

Trying not to alarm her, I suggested that we examine the whole group. Holly handed the puppies to me one by one and I examined them on the kitchen table, checking each one over from head to toe. The only thing I could find was that their abdomens were not as full as they should be. They were just not getting enough to eat. After the puppies, I examined Tara. Her heart, lungs, and temperature were normal, and her mammary glands were still very full of milk. In the center of her abdomen, I thought I could feel something that shouldn't still be there.

Holly piped up, "Well, what do you think? What is the problem?"

"I think that Tara may not have passed everything yet," I told her. "We may need to help her out a little."

I was more than just a little worried what we might find, but Tara desperately needed us to get it out. I would have hated for Holly to see something really bad, though she had seen a lot on the ranch and could probably handle almost anything.

"I'm going to give Tara an injection of oxytocin to help her push out whatever is left in her uterus." As I said this, I imagined the worst scenario: a dead puppy.

Oxytocin is basically the same as Pitocin, the drug used for women to increase uterine contractions during birth. It would be a few minutes before the drug took effect, so Mrs. Hansberger offered Holly and me some chocolate-chip cookies. We both politely passed, too nervous to eat anything at this point. The three of us sat in the living room, staring at one another for what seemed like an eternity. Suddenly, Tara started panting; then her abdominal muscles began to tighten. Still on her side, Tara bore down and gave a big thrust. We held our breath. All three of us were on our knees, staring into the box. Sure enough, out squirted a puppy covered in a shroud of afterbirth. I yanked off the membranes and, much to my surprise, it grunted.

Holly couldn't hold back. "It's alive; it's alive!" she cried.

Mrs. Hansberger handed me an old kitchen towel so I could dry off the little miracle. As soon as I put the puppy back down, nature kicked in, causing the pup to crawl toward mom's teats.

A side effect of oxytocin is the stimulation of milk production, so the other puppies were already wrestling over Tara's leaking nipples. With the rogue puppy out in the world, Tara felt amazingly better. She nearly fell asleep while the pups nursed relentlessly. With all the canines happy, we settled up at the table and I went on my way. The retriever herd escorted me back to the front gate, new father still unaffected by all the trauma inside the house. The Highlanders looked on from a safe distance in their pasture, just glad that I was not there to see them.

The next morning at about seven, I got an emergency page from Mrs. Hansberger. I assumed there was another problem with Tara.

I called, and Holly picked up the phone. "Holly, what's going on? Is Tara having more problems?"

"No, it's worse than that. Let me get Mom." She slammed the phone down on what I was sure was the kitchen table.

I could hear her yell in the background, "Mom, it's the vet!"

She still wasn't happy enough with me to use my name. "The vet" put me into a more temporary category, indicating that I could still be easily replaced. Next came the sound of boot soles shuffling across the old hardwood floor and the clearing of a throat.

Mrs. Hansberger said, "I meant to mention this possibility yesterday, but now it's happened and it's a little more of an emergency."

I girded my loins. What was going on out there that I was going to have to deal with? A period of silence went by, during which I didn't take the risk of speaking, because I didn't really want to know what had gone wrong. The discomfort of me not saying anything forced Mrs. Hansberger to break the uncomfortable silence. "It's Bonnie. She gave birth during the night and we have lost the last two babies." The name Bonnie struck fear throughout most of South Park, or at least with anyone who had helped the Hansbergers with their cattle. She was a medium-sized brown Highlander cow with thin, extra-tall horns. Bonnie was all about attitude, lots of it. Any issues that Harry, the surrogate steer, couldn't deal with, Bonnie would. She had broken at least one neighboring rancher's hand by pinching it between the tip of her horn and a fence board. She was not overly big, but very quick. When upset, she would run with her head as high in the air as she could get it, making her appear larger.

"Her nipples are too swollen with milk for the calf to be able to nurse. This is what has happened in the past. I thought if we could get the calf away from her, I could raise it on a bottle," Mrs. Hansberger said with confidence.

A film clip of bad scenarios played through my head. Nothing about this could be good; someone was apt to get hurt. I asked the inevitable question: "How are we going to do this?"

"Well, they are out in the field, a couple miles from the house. I thought we would try to put our truck between Bonnie and the calf, then get the calf into the bed of the truck." It wasn't really a job that required eight years of college, but they were such nice people, and I would really have hated to see the calf die.

"Okay, I'll be there in about an hour."

It was Saturday, and my wife, Marion, wanted to go with me. I made her promise that she would stay in the cab of the truck, relatively protected from the Highlander's horns. She agreed and we headed for South Park. By the time we pulled into the picturesque ranch, there were other recruits in attendance. One was a young girlfriend of Holly and the other a middle-aged man from down the road who also owned Highlanders. Tom was a small-framed, wiry guy with jet black hair, a matching mustache, and a well-tanned face from the intense South Park wind and sun. He was wearing very appropriate gear for the job—sweatpants and sneakers. Obviously, he'd had prior experience.

We all introduced ourselves; then Tom spoke up with a plan of attack. "What I thought we would do is have Mrs. Hansberger block off Bonnie with the truck; then I will jump out and grab the calf. I will hand the calf to Dr. Wells and I will jump into the back with him. What do you think?"

It sounded as good as anything, and my liability company would be happier that I hadn't come up with it. Mrs. Hansberger and Marion got into the cab of the two-decade-old pickup truck, with the two young girls stuffed in between them. Tom and I climbed into the back as Mrs. Hansberger ground the gears until she found first. With a lurch, we were off.

We started off across the field in search of the unsuspecting cow. Mrs. Hansberger drove at a nice easy pace of only a few miles an hour so as not to bounce Tom and me out of the bed. The fields were criss-crossed with old irrigation ditches for distributing water into the fields. They each were at least a foot deep, which would have made for quite a ride if we'd been going any faster than a few miles per hour.

After about ten minutes, the herd came into sight. Mrs. Hansberger ground the gears until finally finding first again, easing us in like a ship into a minefield. At that point, Tom began to unwrap the rolled-up blanket that lay between us in the truck bed. I had meant to ask him earlier what he had in the blanket, but it had slipped my mind once Mrs. Hansberger cranked up the truck.

Tom saw the curious expression on my face and explained while he lifted the item from its shroud. "We may need this later if Bonnie gets too close or tries to get in the truck with us."

He had to be kidding. It was a rifle—the kind of gun that a lot of ranchers have to protect their stock from bears and coyotes. It looked just like the ones that John Wayne protected the wagon trains with in old black-and-white Westerns.

"There is no way I am going to use it," I blurted. "I can just see it in the local paper: 'Local veterinarian shoots cow.'"

That would be a real business builder. I was supposed to heal animals, not shoot them from the back of a moving pickup truck. It would have been one thing if it were a tranquilizer gun, but this was the real thing. Tom seemed disgusted by my reluctance to use his weapon.

His answer was, "When push comes to shove, you may change

your tunc." I could only hope that he was wrong. I found out later that Bonnie had tried to get into the truck in pursuit of someone before— another one of those things it would have been nice to know before-hand.

Mrs. Hansberger spotted Bonnie on the edge of the herd. She happened to be grazing about twenty feet away from her calf. Our timing was impeccable. Tom started to get excited and whispered to me, "As soon as Mrs. Hansberger gets us between them, I'll jump out. Remember the plan?" Mrs. Hansberger slid the vehicle right between mother and calf.

Holly screamed, "Go now!" and I could see Marion's slightly ter-rified face through the rear window of the cab.

Her expression said, Don't get killed. I normally tried to conceal the day-to-day dangers of my practice from her, especially the large-animal side. Now there was no way to hide the risk.

Tom leaped from the truck, sprinting for the calf, but by now Bonnie had realized what we were up to. Her head popped up. If she could have breathed fire, she would have. Tom grabbed the calf and ran, making it back to the truck just as Bonnie rounded the rear of the vehicle. I pulled the newborn from him just in time for him to launch himself into the bed. Bonnie attempted to follow him in as he scrambled to the front, right behind the cab. The calf and I were positioned there also, as far from Bonnie as possible. The tailgate was down, so she was able to get her head in as she tried to enter.

"Go, Mom." Holly's voice echoed across the field from the pas-senger side, and the pickup lurched forward, with not a moment to spare.

Bonnie looked a bit dazed when we pulled away, but by the time Mrs. Hansberger found second gear, the cow had shaken it off and was after us again. Tom and I both stared at the tailgate. If we could close it, the chances of Bonnie getting in would be a lot less likely. The way it was, if she caught up with us, there was nothing to block her entry.

I turned to the more daring Tom and said, "There is no way we can close it. Way too risky."

Tom replied reluctantly, "You're right. If one of us goes back there to close it and we hit a bump, we're toast."

It was too easy to imagine Bonnie's glee at seeing one of us fall out the back. In her defense, we had kidnapped her calf.

Mrs. Hansberger eventually found third gear, but Bonnie was gaining. It would have been impossible to go any faster, because we were now hitting the irrigation ditches head-on. Tom and I were already bouncing up and down high enough that it hurt each time our rears hit the steel floor of the pickup bed. I tried to keep the calf as stable as possible, but he began bawling for his mother. The newborn's cry for help did nothing but perpetuate its mother's determination. By now we were going about twenty miles per hour, with Bonnie gaining. There was no way to take the ditches any faster, or those of us in the back would have been ejected. Bonnie closed in. She began leaping at the collapsed tailgate, determined to climb into the moving truck. Her tongue was out and she was breathing hard. Tom pulled the gun up onto his lap.

"I may have to use it," he yelled over the rattling truck.

His thumb was on the hammer, ready to cock it. I closed my eyes and hung on. I felt sure this was going to end badly. Instead of the noise I expected to hear, Tom yelled again. "She's giving up! Look."

Sure enough, Bonnie was starting to lag. After nearly a mile, she couldn't keep up anymore. She came to a stop in the field, watching us speed away. I felt a little sorry for her, yet it was the only way for the calf to stand a chance.

"That was close," Tom said as his body relaxed and he wrapped the gun back up.

I, too, began to let my guard down. Even the calf curled up beside me seemed a little less tense and started looking around for some lunch.

Just when we thought we were safe, Holly changed the scene with one word. "Harry!" she screamed.

"Where?" Tom yelled back as he sat straight up.

"Driver's side," she replied.

Sure enough, there he was in all his glory, storming at us with everything he had, his long hair bouncing with every thud of his immense hooves. He had come out of nowhere. It was as if he had taken some kind of shortcut to come to the rescue once Bonnie had given up. He fell in behind the truck, attempting to get in with us just as Bonnie had. Luckily, we had a few more things on our side this time. The calf was too weak from not eating to call to Harry, and we had just driven over the last irrigation ditch. Mrs. Hansberger found fourth gear, leaving Harry in the dust. The ranch was now in sight. We had made it.

On arrival, Marion jumped out, giving me a big hug. She followed it by saying, "You better not be taking this kind of risk on a daily basis!"

Holly's friend, who hadn't said anything the whole time, just looked terrorized and ran for the bathroom. Tom and I got the calf out of the back of the truck, carrying it inside the house. Holly made a bed for it in the kitchen out of old blankets, while Mrs. Hansberger warmed up some milk substitute. Once the large plastic bottle was filled with the warm milk, the little guy sucked the whole thing down in a matter of minutes. At that point, we knew we had done the right thing.

Mrs. Hansberger named the calf appropriately, calling her "Lucky," and raised her into a full-grown pet cow. I still see her every time I go to the Hansbergers' ranch, and she comes up to the fence for me to rub her head or maybe get a treat. But just when I start to get comfortable, I notice Harry in the background, just wishing I would take a chance at rubbing his head.

Nurse Dog

The clientele that walks through the doors of a veterinary clinic is as diverse as in any other business. You never know what kind of personality type you are going to encounter next. Most people are great, but you are always going to have a few who are not going to be as easy. In my experience, clients who work in human medicine are usually great people, yet they can present somewhat of a challenge when it comes to treating their pets.

Mrs. Kurnan's dog, Aspen, was a sweet fourteen-year-old golden retriever with a graying muzzle, stiff hips, and the opaque eyes typically associated with cataracts. Despite displaying all the signs of an aging canine, he was as sweet a dog as one could ask for, always bolting into the clinic with his tail wagging and a sloppy wet lick for any face he could get close enough to. We all loved him and looked forward to his visits. He genuinely seemed to look forward to seeing us, even though he knew that needles often awaited him. Even Christie, who was not overly prone to engaging with the patients in an overt manner, would get down on the floor just to give him hugs. When I picked Aspen up to set him on the exam table, he gave me the obligatory face washing right on cue.

This visit was not a routine one. According to Mrs. Kurnan, Aspen had not been feeling up to par and was not eating with his normal vigor. "He has been PU/PD all week and his mucous membranes are slightly jaundiced," she announced.

Mrs. Kurnan was a nurse at a hospital in Denver. She always came in wearing scrubs, no matter what time of the day it was. I think she did this partly just to remind us that she was a medical person. She also stuck to as much medical terminology as possible. In layman's terms Aspen had been drinking and urinating more than normal, while his gums and eyes had a yellow tinge.

Mrs. Kurnan was in great shape. She was about forty years old and had dyed blond hair and steely blue eyes, which were now staring at me for an answer. She and her husband were bicycle racers, very health-conscious and maybe a little overcompetitive.

After another near tongue kiss from Aspen, I recovered enough to speak. "Well, let's give him a look; then maybe we will want to run a little blood work."

"Well, I would think that you would," Mrs. Kurnan responded. "It would be pretty poor medicine if you didn't."

I held back any comment and proceeded to examine Aspen. I listened to his heart and lungs, then palpated his abdomen and looked in his mouth and ears. I'm sure I subconsciously performed a more thorough physical exam than normal, since Mrs. Kurnan was looking over my shoulder, inspecting my every move.

"Well, I can't find anything visibly wrong other than the jaundice," I said with caution. "So I think we had better go ahead and pull some blood." She nodded her head in approval.

Christie didn't even need to hold Aspen's head as I drew a syringeful of blood from the vein in his front left leg, dodging the infamous tongue the entire time. After I handed Christie the syringe, she filled the appropriate tubes to send them to the lab.

"I will have those results for you tomorrow," I promised Mrs. Kurnan. "We can discuss what to do next then."

"I will need you to fax a copy to me at the hospital as soon as you get them. The doctors I work with can take a look and help me make the proper decision on how to proceed."

I could see that this was going to be fun. Christie and I helped Aspen down from the exam table. He gave us a "Thank you" tail wag

and disappeared out the door with Mrs. Kurnan, who left the hospital fax number with Lorraine on her way out.

The next morning passed quickly. I made a couple of horse calls, arriving back at the clinic around noon. Lorraine met me at the door. "Mrs. Kurnan has called three times, looking for Aspen's blood results. She's not very happy."

"Is Aspen worse today?" I asked with dread in my voice.

"Oh, no," Lorraine informed me. "She said that he was no worse."

All I could think of was that the last time I'd had blood work done at my M.D.'s clinic, I didn't hear from them for over a week. We hadn't heard from the lab yet, so I gave a call and they faxed the results to us in about twenty minutes. As expected, some of Aspen's liver enzymes were high, but not severely so. He also had a slightly high white-blood-cell count, indicating some inflammation. With some antibiotics and a special liver diet, Aspen should do pretty well. Lorraine sent the paperwork on to Mrs. Kurnan. Rookie mistake. I should have called her first.

Within an hour, Mrs. Kurnan was on the phone. "I've had some of my doctors here at the hospital take a look at Aspen's blood work, and they are very concerned. In fact, I would like to have you talk with the hepatologist." How was I ever going to keep up with a human hepatologist when it came to liver disease? All that hepatologists deal with is liver disease. That feeling in the pit of my stomach rushed over me—the same one I used to get when I was fresh out of school and facing a case where I was completely clueless. I ran back to the office, grabbing the overwhelmingly thick book on small-animal medicine off the shelf. A trail of dust followed, resulting in the formation of a cloud over my desk. I figured I needed to crack it open a little more often. I pored over the section pertaining to liver disease in the canine, my eyes straining for anything that I might not have thought of. Could it be a toxin or a bile-duct disorder that I might have missed? Before I could skim through all of the relevant pages, the ring of the phone ended my search. It was like the way a bell at school signals that it is time to put your pencils down and stop the test even though you still have a full page of questions left to answer. I knew that it would be the hepatologist.

A baritone voice bellowed through the phone, "Well, I was looking over the blood work that Nurse Kurnan showed me, and I think that we may want to do some more testing."

I hadn't realized that "we" were now sharing responsibility for the case, but I was listening. "What did you have in mind?" I responded, fearing that he would bring up something that I had never heard about.

"I think that we should do a CAT scan of the liver to check for cancer."

Now, this was before any veterinary clinics that I had heard of had even thought about having a CAT-scan unit available. Sure, it would have been a great idea, but at that time it would have been completely cost-prohibitive for a veterinary clinic, let alone a somewhat rural one like ours.

"So, did you want to do that at the hospital?" I imagined us sneaking Aspen in through the emergency room door, covered up on a gurney.

After a relatively long pause, he said, "You don't have one available even at a nearby veterinary clinic?"

"Ah, no." I waited for him to respond, still hoping to pass Aspen off as a human patient long enough to get him to the CAT-scan machine.

After another long pause, which gave him enough time to think about how he would explain fur or something worse on the floor of the CAT-scan room, he replied, "Why don't you do whatever you feel would be the best for now," and hung up the phone.

Christie put together some antibiotics and pulled out a bag of dog food especially made for those with liver problems. That evening, Mrs. Kurnan came by in her scrubs to pick up the supplies for Aspen.

Lorraine called to me from the waiting room. "Can you talk to Mrs. Kurnan about Aspen?"

Aspen's mom was armed with the copies of his blood work that we had faxed to her earlier. "I would like to go over this blood work with you myself." She plopped down in one of the waiting room chairs, so I sat down beside her.

We went through the paperwork line by line, until she seemed somewhat satisfied. Just when I thought we were done, a tear formed in the corner of her eye. She tried to wipe it away quickly, without my noticing. The tough persona seemed to be melting.

"Are you okay?" I put my hand on her shoulder.

"I'm sorry, I just want to do everything I can to keep from losing Aspen. I want to be sure that I have covered all the bases," she said as she wiped more tears. "My husband and I don't have any children, so Aspen is the closest we have to a child."

I was a bit taken aback. Now that I knew what was really going on behind the facade, she was going to be much easier to deal with. "Aspen is a great dog. We all love him here and want to give him the best care possible, but he is fourteen years old, and we don't want to jump into something like an exploratory surgery, which he might not recover from."

Mrs. Kurnan acknowledged me with a nod. I went on: "So let's start with some antibiotics and a diet change and see how we do." Again, she nodded her acceptance.

I carried the dog food to the car for her, where she squeaked out a "Thank you," then sped off to get Aspen started on his new regimen.

We didn't hear from Mrs. Kurnan for some time after that. I usually consider no news to be good news, but I was beginning to get curious about Aspen's health. Christie had called to follow up and had left messages, yet no one had called her back. Then late one afternoon, Mrs. Kurnan blew in the door just a few minutes before closing. I happened to be standing at the reception desk, filling out a patient chart.

"Oh, I'm so glad I caught you before you closed. I need another bag of that liver diet for Aspen," she announced.

"How is Aspen doing anyway?" I was dying to know.

"He's great, but Dr. James thinks that we should probably leave him on the liver diet. He is afraid that Aspen might relapse if we take him off it."

Dr. James was the human hepatologist who had called me about Aspen previously. Instead of making some sort of snide comment that I might have made as a younger practitioner, I just smiled and imagined Dr. James's human patients leaving his office carrying large bags of canine liver diet.

As Mrs. Kurnan walked back out the door, wearing her scrubs, of course, she got in one more shot. "I'm so lucky to have Dr. James to consult with. I don't know what we would have done without him. I'm sure he will let you call him about other cases, Dr. Wells."

I had to bite my lip until it nearly bled, remembering that the most important thing was that Aspen was doing better. A good rule of thumb for veterinarians is to check our egos at the door of our clinics. It will keep us out of a lot of trouble.

Woman's Best Friend

The end of bachelorhood is often marked by major changes, not the least of which is the inevitable purchase of a home. Most of us survive our premarital years in generic drywall appointments unchanged since their conception. Interior design is not often considered a high priority. In my case, I was lucky enough to rent cabins for a couple hundred dollars a month and furnish them with a couch that I had gotten for vaccinating a dog and a table that I'd had since college. The big surprise was that women usually look for a little something more in a dwelling. Most women are "nesters," and Marion was no exception.

Within a year of our vows, we were cruising our mountain area, looking for the perfect home on a shoestring budget. Like every home hunter, we looked at more homes than we can now remember. The ones we liked were priced more in the range of a hedge-fund manager's salary than that of a young veterinarian. The ones we could afford had driveways that would require a snowcat to access in the winter months.

Our patience had started wearing thin, when I noticed a FOR SALE sign while out on a horse call one day. The house was a very small old cabin with plywood siding disguised by brown paint, but the property was a beautiful five acres. It had towering old ponderosa pine trees and a shimmering aspen grove running down the middle. I pulled a flyer out of the Plexiglas box attached to the metal real estate sign and held my breath as my eyes worked their way down to the price. We could almost afford it, but if the outside of the house was any indication, I was more than a little concerned about what we would find inside the front door.

I drove straight home to the cabin we were renting at the time and presented the flyer to Marion. Surprisingly, the picture of the aging little house didn't scare her off, probably since I tried to focus her attention on the stunning landscape instead. The next morning, we headed over to check the place out. The older woman who was selling the home happened to be outside playing with her new Sheltie puppy and tending to the flowers that grew between the boulders in the front yard. The little dog was squinting its left eye a little and had a drop of white fluid draining from it. I thought it would be a little forward to mention it right away, so I decided to wait until the opportune time. The dog was not a patient of mine and I did not want to appear too pushy.

Mrs. Mitchell had the skin of a woman who had spent a lot of time in the Colorado sun without the protection of sunscreen. A half-smoked cigarette hung from the left side of her mouth and her brownish gray hair was cut short so as not to interfere with her daily activities. We explained who we were and that we were interested in her place, then asked if she could answer a few questions for us.

"Well, I have lived here for almost thirty years and my husband died twenty-five years ago. We had dreamed of building a big new house on the property one day, but obviously plans changed," she said. Her brown eyes welled up a little and she seemed to go to a different place for a brief moment. It was that look of old dreams that, due to life's curveballs, just hadn't worked out the way one had planned.

She went on to tell us how she had raised her two boys in the little house on her own. Not only had she dealt with the usual hardships of a single mother raising two boys alone but she even cut her own wood to heat the cabin. All winter, she had fed the antique woodstove in the living room to save on the heat bill. She was of true pioneer stock.

"I hate to leave all the memories behind, but I have decided to move back to Oklahoma, near where I grew up." Her voice cracked a little before she was able to speak again. "Let me show you inside the house." Her little puppy, who had been nipping at my pant leg the whole time in an attempt to portray a tough guard dog, finally gave in and lay down in the cool grass. He looked rather dejected that his efforts to frighten me off were in vain. I have to admit that his sharp puppy teeth had occasionally punctured my jeans, and my ability to ignore him was starting to wear off. It would have been inappropriate for me to have scolded the pup in front of his owner, whom I had only just met, and it might not have helped with our attempts to buy the property. He was also starting to rub at his eye with his paw. I knew I was going to have to bring it up before we left.

Mrs. Mitchell took one last drag of what was left of her cigarette and threw it on the ground. She then stamped the last bit of life out of it with the heel of her cowboy boot and cracked open the old front door. Before us lay a cavelike living room. There was dark fake-wood paneling on the walls from the early seventies and the windows were covered with heavy woolen blankets. Through the door on the right was the kitchen. *Kitchen* may have been a little bit of an overstatement, but that was what she called it. The living room was primarily taken up by an oversized glassed-in gun case and a ragged couch covered with blankets. In front of the couch, a relatively new fifteen-inch television sat on the floor, from which blared the daily warnings of the Weather Channel.

Two doors led out of the main room, opposite the kitchen. One opened into her bedroom and the other into another tiny bedroom, which, she explained with a smile, "was my boys' room." These rooms had obviously been added to the house in the last fifty years. The walls were drywall and the electrical outlets looked like you might not die if you tried to plug something in. The low ceiling in most of the house consisted of decades-old acoustic ceiling tiles, and the entire floor was, oh yes, covered with green shag carpet—the kind they used to make plastic rakes for.

Marion was hanging in there pretty well until it was time to see the bathroom. It was tucked behind the kitchen and could be accessed through a small, narrow hallway. Now, I had seen some tough bathrooms, having lived with sixty other guys in college, but even I cringed a little. I couldn't look at Marion, but I could feel her tense up as she rounded the corner. Mrs. Mitchell had kept it as clean as possible with what she had to work with, but the thirty-year-old carpet had become a self-contained Petri dish. Yet, it was the shower that stole the show. It was made of metal, and old pipes seemed to shoot out of it from every angle. It had been painted many times over the years and large sections of ancient paint layers hung from inside walls, exposing the rusty metal underneath. I fully expected Marion to cut and run, but she held her ground.

Finally, we headed back outside and started to tour the beautiful property. The puppy seemed to have come back to life, and he led the group with a proud prance. Mrs. Mitchell showed us the projects that she and her husband had done together a generation before—

fences, small buildings, and the spot where they had planned to build a new house. There was even a fenced-in area for a dog. It was almost perfect outside of the cabin, except for one small glitch. Mrs. Mitchell hadn't thrown anything away since the Beatles came to America. There was junk under every tree, and there were a lot of trees. Old car tires seemed as common as pinecones, and her collection of used car batteries was extensive. It was starting to become evident why this property hadn't been snatched up yet. Still, stunning wildflowers were everywhere, and signs that deer and elk had recently been there stuck to the bottoms of our shoes.

We eventually said our good-byes and headed for the car. I suggested that we would be in touch with her Realtor. At that moment, I couldn't stand it anymore; I just had to bring up the puppy's eye. Then, right before I opened my mouth, Mrs. Mitchell piped up. "By the way, since you're a vet, could you take a quick look at my puppy's eye?" I'd thought she would never ask. Marion held the rat-size, squirming pup in her arms while I looked at the sore little eye. I could just make out the end of a tiny weed seed sticking out from the corner of the eye. I fumbled through some instruments in my truck until I found a hemostat, then plucked the irritating seed out from under the eyelid. A little antibiotic ointment and the eye would be as good as new. Mrs. Mitchell thanked me profusely and we were finally on our way.

Holding our smiles together until we were out of sight, we sighed at the same time. We both loved the place, but it would be somewhat like cleaning up a Superfund site. We imagined the place crawling with men in white hazardous-waste suits as they removed truckloads of junk and fumigated the house with big hoses shooting gallons of disinfectant.

We decided to keep looking, but we spent the next month being disappointed at what we could afford. Occasionally, we would drive by Mrs. Mitchell's place to reconsider. Once, we noticed the Realtor was showing the house to another couple. Their brand-new hunter green Land Rover was parked beside the Realtor's Mercedes in the driveway. We turned around at the next house up the road and made another pass. By this time, the wife was already back in the Land Rover. She didn't look like she had just seen her dream house. Eventually, the visions of government cleanup units began to fade, and if we squinted our eyes just right, we couldn't see the old tires and thirty years' worth of trash. We decided to make an offer.

Mrs. Mitchell took us up on it and after a slew of appraisals and negotiations, we closed on the project of our lives. Little did we know that the place was like an iceberg—most of the surprise lay beneath the surface.

The first issue was that Mrs. Mitchell had not moved out by the date she was supposed to, so Marion and I spent the better part of a day loading her belongings into the rented moving truck. I must have missed the "moving the buyer out" clause in the real estate contract. In fact, I haven't heard of a similar situation since, but we were glad to help her out. At last, she settled the pup up on the passenger seat, climbed up behind the steering wheel, waved good-bye, and headed for Oklahoma to start a new life. The fact that a single woman of her age was driving a large truck containing her whole life all the way to Oklahoma was a testament to her strength of spirit. She would be fine.

The next day, I went back to the scene of the crime. This time, I brought along a friend to take a look. Brian and I had gone to veterinary school together back in Iowa. Brian was thin and weighed in at about 140 pounds dripping wet. With my help, he was able to crawl through the small attic opening on the outside of the house. I knew things were not pretty when a muffled voice said, "How much did you pay for this place?" Then he pushed on a random wire and the lights went off in the kitchen. When he emerged from the tiny open-ing, he was covered in a veil of cobwebs that were sprinkled with tiny little black pellets. On closer examination, these turned out to be mouse feces. The attic was literally filled with them. Mrs. Mitchell had not been even close to living alone. It looked like we would not be moving right in. We hadn't had the house inspected, because we already knew it was in bad shape. We just didn't know how bad.

That afternoon, I returned to the rental cabin and announced to Marion, who was packing up in expectation of moving into her new house, that we were going to have to buy a camper to live in while we did "a little fixing up." She said, "No way," but within one week, we had purchased a used camper. A friend with a pickup truck and an appropriate hitch towed it to the new place and we hooked it up with an extension cord to the electricity in the house. This would be our "home" for the next two months.

When we moved into the nineteen-foot-long, six-foot-wide trailer, our family included more than just the two of us. Our newest family member was a ninety-pound female Akita named Rita. Soon after we were married, I had been called out to check on a new litter of Akita puppies—just routine examinations and puppy vaccinations. Marion and I both fell in love with the eight little brown-and-white fur balls. The puppies came from a long line of fancy show dogs and had al-ready been sold to dog-show people all around the country. We had put the pups out of our minds until almost a month later, when I got a phone call at the clinic from the puppies' owner. The voice on the other end of the phone said, "I really don't make this kind of call con-cerning my dogs, but I knew you and your wife really liked my pup-pies. One of the females got in a fight with our neighbor's blue heeler and got an ear hematoma." (A hematoma is a blood blister, which often causes the ear to be permanently deformed.) She paused for a moment

and then continued. "The people who originally wanted her to show don't want her with the damaged ear. Do you think you and your wife would like to have her?" I couldn't get to their house fast enough to pick her up. She was a beautiful dog with a crumpled right ear. It gave her a look of character that we would find out later matched her personality quite well. All this just happened to coincide with Marion's birthday, and just like that, I went from being a big loser with no gift to a wonderful husband with the perfect gift.

Now she wasn't a cute little puppy anymore, but a nearly full-grown canine the size of a small bear, and she wanted to sleep between us in the tiny camper bed. She turned her nose up at the prospect of spending nights in the already-existent pen and small rustic doghouse that came with it. With the three of us now crammed into our temporary home, the work was about to begin.

Standing in the middle of our new living room with no idea where to start, I was armed with only a large hammer and the dream of what the room would look like when we were done. Then, taking a deep breath, I plunged the steel of the hammer through the layers of acoustic tiles, plaster, and who knows what that had been used on this ceiling over the past two-thirds of a century. Then, ramming the claw portion into the hole, I gave a good tug. The floodgates came open. Down came a landslide of antique construction material, followed by oodles of mouse droppings. As luck would have it, I had been looking up at the ceiling with my mouth hanging open. In veterinary school, we had learned about all the diseases that mice carry, and the horrific symptoms came rushing back into my brain. Convinced that certain death was now just around the corner, I interpreted every cough or sneeze over the next few weeks as the beginning of the end. The following morning, I purchased a protective mask and goggles.

The next week, a routine began to develop. Marion and I would both arrive home from work, gobble down a bad microwave meal, and head back into the house to face our nemesis. Marion would head back to the camper by 11:00 P.M., as she had to get up early for work, and I would call it a day at about 2:00 A.M. On top of the late nights and early mornings, the usually arid Colorado summer had turned into the summer of the monsoons. It rained every afternoon—not little drizzles or spring showers, but buckets and barrels every day. The storms were relentless, and, of course, the little camper couldn't withstand it. First, there were just a few drops running down the walls; then we woke up in the night with our blankets soaking wet. We tried caulking the seams and tightening the screws, but nothing seemed to slow down the leak. Our last resort was to cover the whole thing with a blue plastic tarp. It did the job but was a big step backward in our attempt to make the place appear more acceptable.

Eventually, we seemed to have made some real headway on the house. It was still just early August, so we felt we could easily be moved in before the mountains began to turn white. All was good and on course until Marion pulled in the driveway one afternoon in the middle of the daily downpour. She had been to her doctor that morning for a "routine" checkup. Since she'd had cancer and a liver transplant a few years before, she had to have a CAT scan every six months to watch for any recurring tumors. So far, these rechecks had been no big deal, but this time was different. The technicians had kept her longer than usual and repeated some of the scans. We both knew in our hearts what was up, but we avoided talking about it in our quiet camper that night. Even with Rita snuggled in beside us, it seemed a lonely place. We stared at the water-damaged ceiling, with different scenarios running through our heads. No one slept well. Even Rita seemed to toss and turn more than usual. I am sure she could sense our stress. The next morning, the oncologist called Marion at work and then she got hold of me at lunch. I could feel my throat tighten up as her shaking voice gave me the news.

"It's back," she managed to squeak out. "It's in the chest this time. A lymph node near my heart."

The cancer had moved from in and around her liver for a second try in her chest. We both knew all the important structures in this region would make surgery extremely risky. Not to mention that we were living in a camper with a plastic tarp draped over it. Probably not the best place to recover after thoracic surgery.

Now the race was really on! Marion's mother came out from the East Coast and moved into the camper with us. I increased the time I spent working on the house, using every free moment when I wasn't seeing patients. We began to involve friends in the project, recruiting everyone we knew who had a few free hours to give us a hand. Cars on the road by the house would slow down to a crawl to observe the activity, old construction material flying out the front door and new going in. Marion's mother even pitched in, painting and putting down fake tile. If Rita could have used her tongue, she would have pitched in also.

When surgery day came along, the project was just complete enough that Marion could move into the bedroom after her hospital stay. There was still a lot to do, but most of it was superficial. Marion, her mother, and I headed for the hospital at about 5:00 A.M., with Rita looking on as if she wanted to go with us. The hospital staff might have frowned on a ninety-pound dog in the surgery waiting room, but it probably would have been good therapy for all of those involved.

As anyone who has been through this situation knows, the longest hours of your life are those spent waiting for the surgeon to appear to give you a report. You try to prepare yourself for all possibilities, but the minute the doctor comes into the room and pulls off that mask, all bets are off.

This time, the news was good. He felt like he had gotten all of the tumor and Marion had done well throughout the surgery. There would be some radiation treatments to follow, but the worst was over. In a couple days, she was back to the almost-finished house. Marion had decorated the bedroom in cheery, bright colors and finished it off with a new light green bedspread. Now a frail Marion filled up only about one-quarter of the bed; the rest of it was taken up by Rita. She wouldn't leave Marion's side from the minute she got home. It was all I could do to get her off the bed to go outside or to get something to eat. I even had to sleep on the couch. Whenever I would coax her to move, she would just raise one eyebrow, examine me with her big brown eyes, then bury her head deeper into the bedspread. Her eyes were very soulful and wise. They seemed to be telling me that she knew what was best for Marion. Occasionally, she would raise her head and press her moist black nose into Marion's cheek, then give her a couple swipes with her gigantic tongue to make sure she was still okay. Workmen would sometimes have to come through the house to do some finish work on the plumbing or heating system. I was worried that Rita might bite them, or worse, but she would just watch them from her perch in the bedroom. Rita kept visiting hours to a minimum and nobody argued.

Eventually, Marion started to improve and was able to begin moving around. By this time, the house was completed and we could start our lives again. But over the next months, whenever Marion would get tired or not feel well, Rita would be back at her post.

A few years later, we arrived home from a day off and found Rita dead in her doghouse. Her stomach had twisted, a common occurrence among large-breed dogs. We were both devastated. Our large furry companion of eight years was gone so quickly. We hadn't had any time to prepare or say good-bye, but, on the other hand, she hadn't suffered long. There was an immediate void in our world. Such a big part of our lives was missing, and we consoled ourselves by reminiscing about all the good times we'd had with her and about her role as nurse and protector after Marion's surgery. We were blessed to have had such a wonderful friend.

I felt we should bury her that evening, so we wrapped her in her favorite blanket, gently placed her body in a wheelbarrow, and transported her to the far end of the property, where I would dig her grave. Digging at 8,500 feet in the Rockies is not as easy as you might think. The job not only required a shovel but also a pickax, which was necessary to break up the rocks along the way. The topper tonight was that it was Halloween and there was a full moon. Marion had her work cut out for her distracting the trick-or-treaters from noticing the man swinging the pickax in the moonlight.

I chose a spot under the protective boughs of an immense ponderosa pine and I worked until the rock at the bottom of the hole became too thick to break up. Then, fighting back the tears, I lowered Rita's body onto the granite floor of her grave and secured the blanket around her. After placing her favorite toy, an old ragged teddy bear, next to her head, I said my good-byes and began to shovel the dirt back in. As an extra precaution to prevent wildlife from getting into the grave, I gathered rocks to place over the top of the site. The work was almost done when I stumbled onto a large flat rock about a foot and a half in diameter. Quickly brushing the dirt off, I placed it in the headstone position at one end of the grave. Then, stepping back, I caught a glimpse of the big stone in the soft moonlight. To my disbelief, it was in the shape of an almost-perfect heart.

Elvis

During a busy summer, it's easy to put off things that are not an emergency or that do not seem like an emergency in my eyes. The risk of procrastinating in these cases is that such matters can quickly become urgent, especially for the humans involved. This time, it was the owners of the local guest ranch—the same one where a young cowboy had received a burro hoof in the groin a couple years before—who were on the phone asking for me. They had purchased a new pet burro, but this time it was a miniature and it had not yet been neutered. They had been anxious to get this procedure done, as miniature male burros tend to have more than their allotted share of bravado. They will often announce their presence by braying nonstop at maximum volume while parading around like a frat boy on sorority row. Now they had paying guests there for the summer and the burro was waking them up by starting his chorus at sunrise. I was sure that this was the issue they were calling about.

"Hey, Melanie, how are things going?"

"Jeff, we have to get that burro fixed. He has picked out one of the mares and is pestering her constantly." She seemed a little agitated with me for not getting this procedure done sooner.

"I am sorry. It's been a hectic summer, but I will try to get there in the next couple weeks," I promised her.

"Okay, as soon as you can. I really like the little guy, but he is becoming downright irritating." She hung up, and I told Lorraine that we needed to put them on the schedule as soon as possible.

A week after the phone call, Christie and I gathered our equipment and headed to the ranch to perform the surgery. It was a beautiful sunny day, perfect for a field surgery, but since it was late July, an afternoon rainstorm was imminent. When we arrived, we found they had a few other cases lined up for us to evaluate first. Three horses were lame and one poor old fellow needed a tooth removed in order to eat and keep his weight on. By the time we worked up the lameness cases and pulled the decaying tooth from the old gelding, the clouds had started to build over the peaks. The ranch didn't have a safe covered area where we could perform the surgery, so when the first cracks of thunder rumbled off the rocky cliffs that surrounded us, Christie gave me the "Let's get out of here now!" look. "I think we had better wait to work on Elvis until another day," I said. Christie would have left me behind if I hadn't come to this decision. Elvis was the name the wranglers had bestowed on the aggressive little burro, and it seemed appropriate.

Another week plus passed, during which Elvis faded from my immediate list of cases—that is, until Lorraine received another, more agitated call from Melanie. The story as relayed to me was that Elvis was now trying to follow his favorite mare out on rides. The girlfriend in this case was a horse named Cadillac, who, fortunately, was an experienced trail horse and not frazzled by this obsessive crush. Unfortunately, her rider was much more concerned about this budding romance. The rider, a rather intense fashion designer from New York, was more than a little upset about having her mount constantly followed by the lovesick creature. It was only Monday, and the concerned guest was already threatening to leave early without paying if the harassment kept up. There was no way that I could make it up to the ranch on Tuesday, so I promised Melanie that we would be there on Wednesday for sure.

"Lorraine, block out the whole morning on Wednesday for a burro surgery," I purposely yelled to her while Melanie was still on the phone. I wanted her to know that I was committed.

"Got it down, Doc," Lorraine yelled back, loudly enough that Melanie could hear her response.

"Okay, great," Melanie said. "I'll plan on seeing you then. Otherwise, I'm going to have to call someone else."

That comment didn't leave me with a good taste in my mouth. I'd always prided myself on providing good customer service, but this time I had dropped the ball. At best, it could cause the ranch to lose money if the lady left early. At worst, someone could get hurt.

Wednesday, I arrived at the clinic a few minutes early to pack up the necessary equipment so that we could get to the ranch in plenty of time. I clearly needed to make up for my procrastination. Christie arrived right at eight and we took off for the ranch.

"Do we have enough anesthetic?" I nervously asked Christie from behind the wheel.

"Yes, I checked it all yesterday before I went home. As long as you didn't have to knock out six horses last night after I left, there is more than enough. Why are you so paranoid?" She seemed a little frustrated with me, too.

"Oh, I just feel bad that we put this off and that Melanie is a little upset."

She raised one eyebrow before responding. "What is this 'we' stuff? I'm not sharing the blame for this." I nodded my head in agreement and we continued for several minutes without speaking as we followed the river through the narrow canyon to the ranch. Now I had everybody mad at me.

Finally, Christie broke the silence. "Look, it's all going to work out fine. We'll get Elvis taken care of this morning; then he won't bother any mares again."

"You're right. Thanks for trying to make me feel better."

It really didn't help at the time, but it was nice of her to try. She rolled down her window, letting the mountain air blow through her hair as we turned off the highway for the last leg of our trip.

I pulled through the gates of ranch and down the narrow drive to the corral. Christie jumped out of the truck, opening the gate for me to pull in. A pair of young summer ranch workers stood in front of me, dressed in cowboy clothes that they had probably purchased right after they flew in from college.

"Are you guys ready to get Elvis taken care of?" I asked. But instead of responding, one of them just nodded in the direction of the driveway that we had just come down.

I turned, to see Melanie walking briskly toward us, arms folded across her chest. By the time I turned back to the cowboys, they had scattered. This was not good. Something bad must have happened, I thought. Melanie was a thin brunette in her mid-thirties, with muscular arms from all the hard physical work at the ranch. She was wearing her typical summer outfit: a sleeveless western-style shirt with Wrangler-brand jeans. What was missing on this visit was her usual broad, welcoming smile. In its place was a forbidding frown. Christie stayed out of range as Melanie pulled up in front of me.

"Well, you are a little too late, but go ahead and get the surgery done today as long as you're here. The guest whose horse Elvis has been harassing has left." Melanie looked right through me as she spoke. "She was pretty angry and won't be very good advertising for us back in New York."

She continued with the account of events on Tuesday that had led up to the lady's departure. Evidently, the lady was coming back from an all-day trail ride with a group of other riders. Melanie had stepped out of the office to wave to them and ask them if they had a good time, when Elvis came running up from the corral. The staff had tried to keep him penned up until I was able perform his surgery, but he was too sneaky and managed to squeeze between the rails of his confines. He headed right for Cadillac, taking his obsession one step further. He jumped onto one of Cadillac's rear legs, and the rest was self-explanatory. Now keep in mind that the lady from New York was still astride Cadillac as this was taking place. Evidently, she let out a bloodcurdling scream, demanding that someone get her off the horse. Melanie dived for Elvis in an attempt to extricate him from

the mare, but Elvis was determined and grasped hold of Cadillac with both of his front legs. With the help of some staff members, Melanie was eventually able to separate Elvis from his true love. The woman was helped down off of Cadillac, only for her to run to her cabin to pack for the airport.

By the time that Melanie had finished her story, Christie and I were losing the battle to all-out laughter. Snickers also came from behind the barn, were the corral staff was still hiding. Even Melanie couldn't hold back. "I really wanted to be mad, but as I told the story, I began to realize how funny it was. That lady was kind of a problem anyway. She didn't like any of the food and was not a favorite among the other guests." She sighed. "You probably did us all a favor by not showing up sooner."

Melanie turned and strolled back up the driveway, whistling as she went. Christie and I proceeded to perform the surgery, and Elvis recovered nicely. He stopped waking the guests up early and never embarrassed Melanie again. He continued to greet the trail riders when they came back to the ranch. He would proudly escort Cadillac back into the corral, but never with the vigor that he had had on that X-rated Tuesday afternoon.

Alpaca Down

It had been a few years now since I had been knocked to the ground by the Linns' horse, who thought it would be fun to put his hoof in my groin. I had treated their animals many times over the next few years, and the flashbacks from that day had finally started to fade. They called one morning about 7:45, and I had already finished my first call by that time. I had been pulled out of bed earlier that morning by a cow with a bad case of gas buildup. Having spent the previous hour relieving the bovine bellyache by placing a long plastic tube down the animal's throat, I was now wide-awake. The smell of fermenting grass and grain from the stomach of a cow will wake you right up. This combination could potentially put Starbucks right out of business.

The Linns had decided about a year before to go into the alpaca business. They had purchased about a dozen pregnant alpaca females, with the hopes of growing the herd and raising them for their hair. The plan was to shave the alpacas at least once a year; then Mrs.

Linn would make sweaters to sell. They had even purchased a loom to weave the sweaters. She was probably not going to be the next Martha Stewart of alpacas, but they seemed very determined to make it work.

On that morning, Mrs. Linn sounded like she thought it was too late to save one of her alpacas. It was down and not looking so good. "I'm not sure that she is still alive. Let me go check real fast." She put down the phone while she ran back outside. About a minute later, she returned and picked up the receiver again. "Well, she's still breathing, but she is flat out on her side in the grass. I guess you had better hurry if you are going to come."

Unfortunately, the Linns still lived in the same location, a rather remote area surrounded by national forest. I had just arrived back home when the call came in, and as much as I wanted to take a shower, I had to go right back out.

I sped down the gravel road leading to the Linns' and barely missed at least one pickup truck traveling in the opposite direction. People in rural areas tend to drive down the middle of back roads, thinking that they are going to be the only ones on them. It was a beautiful morning drive. The sun shone through the pine trees, painting the road ahead with stripes of alternating bright light and shadows, much like a strobe light flashing. Pulling into the Linns' driveway and past the ALPACA CROSSING sign nailed to a ponderosa pine, I saw Mrs. Linn standing just outside of her beautiful new log home, motioning for me to keep coming. She must have cashed in some family money to pay for that, I thought as I pulled up past the house and into the open pasture on the other side. In the middle of the grassy field lay the sprawled-out body of the young female alpaca. She was beautiful, with large brown-and-white spots formed by long hair that covered her body. A long red nylon lead rope was strung out in front of her and a shiny brass snap attached it to the matching halter on her head. Mrs. Linn had been trying to get the animal up before I arrived. As I knelt by her limp body, it appeared that life had almost left her.

"Is she still with us?" asked Mrs. Linn, looking over my shoulder.

It took me a minute to make myself believe that I had seen her chest rise a quarter of an inch, just enough to convince me she was still alive. "Well, she is alive, but not very," I replied with caution. "I am afraid that she won't be for long."

Given the size of her udder, it was obvious that she had been nursing a baby. If we lost her, we would most likely lose the baby, which Mrs. Linn had carefully locked in the barn while we checked over his mother.

On further examination, I could hear a faint heartbeat through my stethoscope. Her pupils were still constricted from the bright sunlight. Fixed, dilated pupils are not consistent with life, so this was a good sign. Mrs. Linn brought up the inevitable question. "Is there anything we can do?"

I didn't feel that there was much that we could do, yet I had to try something. My alpaca medicine was at least as bad as my llama medicine, but certain conditions seem to cross the species barrier fairly consistently.

"I think that her blood sugar may be low from producing milk for her baby. She seems to be so worn down that her body is eating away at itself to maintain milk production."

I tried to speak with much more confidence than I actually had. There was no time to bring in an alpaca specialist. "We need to try some intravenous glucose, but I really think it is probably too late." I'm not usually so discouraging, but I wanted her to realize what bad shape the patient was in. Mrs. Linn wanted to go ahead and make a last-ditch attempt. She headed for the house to call her husband and

fill him in. I went to my truck for needles, syringes, and glucose solution. There wouldn't be a need for anyone to hold the patient while I gave the injection. She wasn't going anywhere.

After rifling through my truck for the nearly expired glucose solution, I turned to my dying patient, who was now standing up on all four legs, staring at me. This can't be, I thought. She must have an identical twin in the pasture. I scanned the pasture, but we were the only two in it. Once I'd convinced myself that she wasn't a ghost, I reached out to grab her lead rope. The second she felt pressure on her halter, she took off, running circles around me because I still held the lead. She bucked and pulled, even attempted to throw herself on the ground in order to get away from me. I wondered what Mrs. Linn would think when she discovered me playing tug-of-war with her near-death female alpaca. The determined animal continued to put up this fight for a couple minutes, during which time I was concentrating too much on just holding on to notice that we were inching across the field. The revitalized alpaca was manipulating me in the direction that she wanted. Before I knew it, she had dragged me to a small stack of hay bales shoved up against the side of the small barn. When she reached her goal, she began devouring the closest one more like a starving dairy cow than a cute little alpaca mother who only minutes ago appeared to have already had her last meal. Now she was ripping and tearing at the hay with the tenacity of a prehistoric raptor.

"It's a miracle! What did you do to save her?" I had been so dumbfounded by the eating frenzy that I hadn't noticed Mrs. Linn approaching. "Seriously, what happened?"

As much as I wanted to tell her how my treatment had worked instantly, just as I'd known it would, I couldn't bring myself to do so. "Well, I really don't know what happened," I replied honestly. "One minute she was practically taking her last breath and the next minute this." I conveniently left out the part about how a nearly expired alpaca had dragged me around the pasture.

"However it happened, I can't thank you enough." Mrs. Linn then gave me a big hug before throwing open the barn door to let the baby out.

The adorable little creature made a mad dash for his mom, then, after a split-second reunion, dived in for a much-needed meal. All you could see was the little guy's rear end, his tail wagging at lightning speed. I suggested a diet for the mother that would help prevent a relapse of hypoglycemia, which I thought had been the cause of her lethargy, and headed out to try to get that shower again.

As I drove down the driveway, Mrs. Linn yelled to me, "Thanks again, and send us a bill right away."

This was one of those times that I wouldn't be sending a bill. What would I put on it? That despite my lack of knowledge in alpaca medicine, this one had somehow survived? The lesson for me, which I have relearned several times during my practice, is how strong the will to survive is, especially when there is an offspring to care for. I never gave up on my patients as easily again.

Maternity Ward

The highway at four in the morning was completely devoid of cars, but I was not at all alone. Pairs of reflective eyes peppered the shoulder on both sides of the road, occasionally dashing across the pavement in front of me as if playing highway Russian roulette. The last thing I wanted to do was hit an animal while on my way to save another. It was a stretch of mountain road that was well known for its deer/automotive encounters, but it was the only route to the emergency call that lay ahead.

Horses with birthing problems are among the top ten most dreaded situations for veterinarians. These situations can end badly for both the mare and foal even in the best of circumstances. The voice on the phone had said, "The head is coming, but I can't see any feet or legs." The usual presentation should be the feet first, followed quickly by the nose. I held out hope that those feet would miraculously be showing by the time I arrived.

After several miles of deer dodging, I arrived at the Mansons' place, turning off the highway and going up the steep driveway. The house and barn stood on the side of a hill steep enough that if you missed the turn on one of the two switchbacks, you would not stop rolling until you hit the highway again. The Mansons' home had originally been part of a mining camp in the early 1900s, explaining its perched position on the hill. The barn had once been a miner's shack. It was made from the trees that had stood on this rugged mountainside over a hundred years ago. Now the logs that made up its walls had empty spaces between them where the chink had once been. A skeleton of its former self, the roof, or what was left of it, held on for dear life as the wind whipped across the old homestead.

Laura Manson met me at the truck before I could even get the door open. Her young face appeared a little terrorized. "It doesn't look good. Maggie is down and the foal's tongue is purple," she blurted. Laura was the daughter of the current owners of the property. At twenty-five, she was a fairly attractive young woman with long brown hair and a round, happy face. She had grown up on the side of this hill, and it had made her strong and tough for her age. She had seen both new life and death before, but she hoped this morning it would not be the latter. Laura had raised horses here her whole life, so she was familiar with the issues we were facing.

"Well, let's take a look and see what we are dealing with," I said as we moved toward the barn. I tried to conceal my uncertainty, dreading the job that lay ahead. If this was going to be easy, that mare would have had the foal herself. The fact that she needed my assistance meant that she had given up and it would not be quick or easy.

Inside the barn, the scene had unfolded much as I had feared. The gray mare lay on her side, with the little black head of a foal sticking out the way it was supposed to, except there were no feet to be seen. Maggie, the mare, was exhausted from trying to push out a foal that had its front legs stuck somewhere behind her pelvis. I stroked her sweaty neck and could see the anxiety in her large brown eyes. Ideally, with a horse having this severe a birthing issue, I would have stabilized her and sent her to a referral equine hospital in the city. But this mare was in no shape to make the trip. Neither she nor the foal would have stood a chance of surviving the hour-plus trailer ride. I was going to have to make do with what I had in the truck and some moonlight.

I fought the panic creeping up inside me. It might seem to the outside observer that one would tug on the head of the baby and it might just slide right out. If it could only have been that simple. The foal's front legs would have to be repositioned and pulled out before any attempt to pull the entire baby horse out could be initiated. I could still picture the demonstration that one of my veterinary professors, Dr. Icorino, had given on equine birthing problems. He was a short brick of a man, with huge hairy arms and a balding head. "A mare can break your arm just by the contractions of her uterus pushing your arms against her pelvic bone," he had announced with some satisfaction. Imagining one of my arms giving in to the pressure and snapping inside of a horse always made me shiver, which was one of the many reasons why I would be anesthetizing Maggie for this procedure. The horse that Dr. Icorino had demonstrated on had been brought into the school with a problem similar to the one I was staring at this morning. With his years of experience and superhero arms, Dr. Icorino had still strained, sweated, and sworn a little before the foal slid out onto the sterile concrete floor of the teaching hospital. How was I going to make this happen without even the help of a trained technician?

I evaluated my surgical suite. The wind funneled between the logs and a tiny bit of moonlight shone through the "skylights" formed by holes in the roof. My staff was made up of Laura and her boyfriend du jour, Shane, who was squatting in the far corner. He was a thin young man in his early twenties, sporting skintight Wrangler jeans, a shabby leather jacket, and worn brown cowboy boots with patched toes. He just gave me a quick skeptical glance from under his filthy gray cowboy hat, then dropped his gaze back to the dirt floor and spat a glob of chewing tobacco a few inches out in front of him. This act appeared to reflect his opinion of my being there. He probably thought he would have been a better candidate to remove the impinged foal. His apathetic response would accelerate his demise. It was unlikely that Shane would still be around the next time I came to the Mansons'.

Laura tried to make up for her boyfriend's attitude and called out, "We are ready and willing to help, Doc, in any way we can. Right, Shane?" She slowly turned back to me again and through clenched teeth asked, "What can we do?"

I mentally started to work myself through the procedure. I would need to anesthetize the mare, rub lots of lube onto my arms, and reach into her uterus. The next step would be, hopefully, to pull those front legs back out into a normal position before pulling the foal free from its mom.

"Laura, if you would sit by the mare's head and try to keep her calm, I'll grab some drugs and equipment from the truck. Shane can assist me in repositioning the foal."

This comment finally got his attention and brought him to his feet. His tough-guy persona seemed to fade a bit. I don't think he had actually thought he would have to get messy.

In the truck, I pulled out the necessary anesthetic and dug out the nylon straps that would be used to pull the legs of the foal forward. A gallon jug of lubricant and long plastic obstetrical sleeves finished off the list of items that would be required for this task. Heading for the soft light coming from the small door of the old barn, I fantasized that a miracle had occurred while I was out at the truck. Maggie would have given a magical push, causing the foal to come shooting out, alive and full of vigor. Of course, this had not happened. I was going to have to suck it up, dig in, and relieve this poor mare.

I patted her neck and injected her jugular with sedation to begin the relaxation process. Laura held the mare's head in her lap and caressed her ears. "It will be better very soon and you won't feel anything. Dr. Wells will get your baby out and both of you will be fine," she whispered. Little did she know how many things had to go right for this to happen, on top of the fact that I was not overly experienced with equine birthing issues.

I injected the second syringeful of medication into the jugular vein. This was the one that would slip her into sleep and keep her out of pain temporarily. As I knelt down at the rear of the sleeping horse, the wind pelted my face with stinging flakes of snow. My whole body tightened in defense.

The foal was starting to weaken. Its tongue had swollen too much to retract it into its mouth and its eyes were beginning to glaze over a little. Its swollen tongue was the result of the pressure of the birth canal around the baby's neck, impeding blood flow. The brown coat was drying out, along with the mother's membranes. I pulled the blue plastic obstetrical gloves over my hands and arms, then dumped a copious amount of lubricant into my left palm. I smeared the lube around the edges of the birth canal next to the foal, so it would be easier for me to slide my arms in to manipulate the foal's legs.

I slid my right hand between the foal and the mare's pelvis, reaching back to grasp for a hoof. The pressure of the foal's shoulder and the bony pelvis of the mare pinched my forearm so intensely that my fingers almost immediately went numb. My swelling fingers continued to fish for the elusive tiny hoof. I pulled back just a little, then used my body weight to push my arm an inch or two farther into the mare's uterus. My fingers were beginning to tingle as the feeling drained from my hand. The space was just too tight, but I still had one more weak attempt left in me. The backs of my knuckles bumped against something harder than the surrounding tissue. It was a hoof. I would have to move it out beside the head without tearing the fragile uterus. I pulled my arm outside the mare and sat back on my knees, breathed deeply for a minute, and then worked the blood back into my hand. What I needed was another set of hands to tug on the pulling straps while I guided the tiny legs to freedom.

"Shane, I'm going to need you to help me get these legs pulled out." This seemed to shock him out of his apparent state of boredom. He flashed me a look that screamed, Look, buddy, I am not here to do any actual work or get dirty!

"I can't get this foal out without your help, so are you in or not?"

Laura piped up, "Please help him, Shane. The baby won't live much longer if we don't get it out soon." Shane finally shrugged and got his narrow body moving in my direction.

With Shane now looking over my shoulder, I lubed up my sleeved arm again, grabbed the looped end of the pulling strap, and, holding on to it, delved back in between the foal and the mare's pelvis. I inched my weakening fingers along between the mare's uterus and the foal. All the tips taught back in those reproduction classes played back through my mind.

"Don't puncture the uterus with your fingers. When you find the hoof, cup it in the palm of your hand to protect the uterine wall."

This wonderful advice seemed less than helpful, as my arm was becoming paralyzed and I hadn't even found the hoof again. No advice had been included on how to revive your weakening limp arm in the snow. Just when I thought that my arm had nothing left, my fingernails tapped that elusive little hoof again. I allowed myself to have my own little celebration inside my head, but I stifled any outward emotion. Better to just lead onlookers to believe that I was completely confident and I would not have expected the procedure to have progressed any other way. After my little mental party, I got just enough length out of my arm to work the looped end of the strap over the hoof. The next step would require the help of my expressionless assistant.

"Okay, Shane, when I say so, pull steadily on the end of that strap."

He grunted back at me, a response that I was beginning to accept as the best I would get. I cupped my protective hand around the hard little hoof.

"Now pull gently, Shane," I whispered.

Somehow, my subconscious must have believed that if I whispered, he would not jerk the strap or pull too hard. He actually did a pretty good job. I was able to guide the hoof as he pulled the lower leg forward. It popped out of the birth canal beside the foal's head just as it should have in the beginning.

"Good job, Shane. Now we have one more to get before we can introduce this little guy into the world."

I lubed up again and we repeated the same drill with the other leg. The foal tried to pull this one back a couple of times, but it was too weak to give us much of a challenge.

Now with both front feet in the correct position, it was time to get the foal out before we lost him. My fingers never seem to work as well when I am in a hurry. They fumbled as I tried to attach the pulling straps to both feet. The fact that they were covered with fluids and obstetrical lube didn't make the situation any easier. Finally, the loops at the ends of the straps found their target over the tiny hooves.

"Time to pull, and this time we have to be fast," I announced.

Under his breath, Shane whispered, "Now he wants to hurry."

I wasn't sure whether I was supposed to have heard that or not, but I decided to ignore the comment in the interest of the fading foal. We each pulled on our respective straps, causing the baby to let go of the womb and begin sliding into the world. Simultaneously, we each sucked in a big breath, leaned into the straps, and gave a last big tug. The next thing we knew, we were both on our butts in the frozen manure that carpeted the shed's floor. The foal was struggling for air in front of us, covered in placenta and gasping for breath, but

she was alive. Laura leaped from her position at the mare's head to tear the uterine membrane from the foal, allowing her to breathe more easily. I shook myself, got up, grabbed some of the scant straw from the floor, and started drying off the foal. Laura grabbed a handful and joined in. Newborn animals respond well not only to being dried off but also to the stimulating effect of the rough straw. It raises the wet hair up off the skin while awakening the nerve endings. Laura knew this, and she rubbed the foal furiously to get her up and running. She also knew the other trick—take a long piece of straw and stick it down into one of the nostrils. It seems like a rude thing to do to a newborn, yet it is often lifesaving. The little creature will cough and sneeze out any fluids left in the sinuses, thereby opening the airways and making air intake a lot easier.

Shane stood over us with his hands in his pockets. "What are you guys doing?"

Laura lashed back at her less than brilliant significant other. "We are trying to save this baby. Maybe you could help."

Shane sighed, then resentfully dropped to his knees in a lame attempt to help. I don't think this was how he had planned to spend these morning hours, and judging by the look on Laura's face, they would not be spending a whole lot more time together.

Suddenly, the traumatized foal snorted and shook herself off. Our resuscitation work had paid off. Her breathing became deeper and more regular. She even attempted to stand. Watching a new foal try to stand can be a humorous yet pitiful situation. A foal's legs are so long for its body that they look almost cartoonlike. The reason for these extraordinary appendages was that originally, in the wild, they could cover a lot of ground quickly to escape predators. The only problem with this is that newborn horses have to raise themselves up on these stilts before they can run. She tried getting up on her back legs, then her front legs, then collapsed on them like a spider. She just didn't have enough energy left to pull it off.

With all the excitement surrounding the birthing, I had completely forgotten about the mare. The anesthesia had almost worn off and she was starting to make the low whinny sound that horses make only when talking to their babies.

"Laura, could you calm mom down?" I asked. "I'm going to have to tube her foal with some colostrum to get her jump-started."

Laura nodded, moving toward the mare's head. She knew the importance of the colostrum, or first milk. The first milk that mammals produce contains an extra-high concentration of proteins, fat, and antibodies to help fight off infection. It's like liquid gold to a newborn. Colostrum gives them energy and can make a dying baby do a 180. Unfortunately, in these types of situations, the foals are usually too weak to take the milk themselves. They often have to be given the milk through a nasal gastric tube. "Shane, keep rubbing down the foal and I will be right back with a tube." I got a Shane grunt in response. I took that for a yes and headed for the truck.

It took a few minutes digging around in the truck before I came up with a tiny polyethylene tube and a stainless-steel cup to collect the milk in. I returned to the barn, knelt down beside the mare's udder, and started squeezing out the thick colostrum into the cup. The mare objected a little by raising her back right leg, but she then relaxed it quickly in submission. She seemed to know I was attempting to help her daughter. After filling the cup, I poured the contents into a large syringe and handed it to Shane. He appeared completely disgusted by the warm contents, but he held on to it with two fingers and turned up his nose.

"After I run the tube down the baby's nose into the stomach, you will attach the syringe to the end of the tube and slowly push it in," I explained.

He appeared worried about his new responsibility, but he didn't do anything to indicate he wouldn't play along. I threw a leg over the foal's chest and eased her onto her side. Then, holding her head gently, I passed the tube through her nostril to the stomach, blowing on the end of the tube the whole time to keep the esophagus open as the tube descended. Once it was in the stomach, I motioned to Shane, and he attached the milk-filled syringe to the tube. "Now push in the milk very slowly. We don't want to rupture anything" A little annoyed at being told twice, he began dispensing the lifesaving fluid.

It seemed like only seconds after all the milk was in and the tube was removed that the patient perked up. She shook herself off again, then proceeded to stand up. Of course, she immediately tipped over on her side, but on her second try, she managed to stay upright. Laura let out a squeal and clapped. Even Shane raised his eyebrows, indicating his approval. The mare lifted her head, relieved to see her baby standing.

Now it was time to get the mare up. She had been down for a long time, and horses can sustain muscle damage if down for too long. Their weight is too much if they stay on one side for extended periods of time. Laura steadied the mare's head while I held on to her tail. Shane slapped her on the side and we coaxed her onto her feet. She was a little wobbly at first, but we held her steady until she could get her sea legs. In a few minutes, she felt comfortable enough to nuzzle her new baby, pushing the little one in the direction of her udder to nurse.

By now, just enough early-morning light had crept in between the old logs for us to see that both mom and baby were going to make it. The yellow light glinted off the slick, damp coat of the foal, who was sucking down milk with a vengeance. Hearing the squeaking sound made by the nursing foal was the best-possible reward we could have had. It even helped us temporarily forget how exhausted we were.

Laura walked me out to the truck, giving me a quick hug. "I just can't thank you enough," she whispered. Glancing over her shoulder, I could see Shane rolling his eyes and looking less than elated.

Laura saw me looking in his direction and whispered in my ear again. "Don't worry, he won't be here next time."

I slipped into the truck seat, cranking the heat as high as it would go. Waving smugly at Shane, I let the steep driveway lead the truck out onto the highway, where the sun planted itself directly in the middle of the windshield. Squinting my eyes, I was able to make out the center line just well enough to stay on my side of the road. My mind was clogged with visions of a shower, followed by the possibility of a quick nap. As tired as I was, at least the patients were doing well and I didn't have any broken parts. There are worse ways to start a day.

What Makes a Vet

One of the most common questions people ask me, and probably ask most veterinarians, is "What made you become a veterinarian?" The answers are probably as varied and as numerous as the practitioners themselves. Most of our answers entail a love of animals from an early age, often coinciding with a lack of interest in dealing with humans, or at least a less than perfect ability to do so. My answer fits partially into this mold, but a particular event pushed me over the edge.

On the hobby farm that I grew up on in Iowa, our menagerie of pets included a small herd of sheep. This group included ten ewes and one ram. The ewes were basically calm and fun to be around, while the male, like most unneutered male livestock, could have an extremely bad attitude. We named ours Ben, short for Big Ben. At well over two hundred pounds, he had a large, boulderlike head to back up his demeanor. Getting hit by a skull like his would not only knock down a large man but might break bones or rupture a spleen. My dad had built a special corral for Ben so we could feed, water, and open and close the pasture gate without actually getting in with him. The gate was an engineering feat in itself. We could stand on the outside of the fence, pulling on a rope that, after running through a couple of pulleys, would swing the gate to the pasture open so he could fill his belly with grass. A strategically placed counterweight then closed the gate behind him. The whole procedure was repeated when it was time to put him back into his pen. This was an awful lot of investment for an animal that had to work for only a short time each year. For all his faults, he was a beautiful creature and produced great lambs, which were born strong and grew quickly. This brings us to the reason for my story.

It was March in Iowa, the time when many farm animals give birth. Our ewes were bursting at the seams and lambs were being born left and right. We had set up the barn with individual lambing pens constructed with freshly painted white gates and stuffed with bright yellow straw. Standing in the clean straw were contented mothers, who were encouraging their lambs to nurse, and others ewes, who were waiting to have lambs. The only noise in this bucolic scene was the constant munching of sweet-smelling alfalfa hay. It was exciting to get home every afternoon from fifth grade and run to the barn to see if any new lambs had been born that day. This routine was a lot of fun until the day I showed up at the barn and discovered a major problem. One of the older ewes was lying on her sternum, breathing hard and obviously in distress. On closer examination, my worst fears were confirmed. She was halfway through giving birth. The head and two feet were protruding, but the lamb was extremely large and it seemed to be stuck on its pathway into the world. Unfortunately, by the look of things, the ewe had been trying to push this baby into the world for some time and the situation was becoming urgent. She looked up at me as if to say, It's about time someone got here. She didn't realize that your average fifth-grader was not really going to be a lot of help.

I had seen several animals born, but I'd never participated in a problem birth. Spurred on by the false relief caused by my arrival, the anxious mother returned to her attempt to expel the lamb. She rolled onto her side, laid her head back onto the straw, closed her eyes, and strained with all she had. The poor thing kept this up for about three minutes, while all I could do was watch helplessly. I eventually just dropped to my knees, holding her head in my lap. I rubbed her forehead between the ears and talked softly, trying to ease her pain without sounding panicked.

"Easy, girl. We can do this," I whispered, as if I was in any way helping. Her head went limp in my lap and she panted relentlessly to catch her breath. This scenario repeated itself four or five times, until I couldn't take it anymore. I had to do something. I placed the ewe's head gently back on the barn floor and pushed extra straw under it. "I will be back as fast as I can," I promised, and sprinted the eighty yards from the barn to the house. I tore into the kitchen and dived for the phone.

"Veterinary office," came the voice on the other end. "How may I help you?"

I replied, breathing heavily, "I have a lambing emergency. Can someone come?"

There was a pause and some two-way-radio noise in the background; then the receptionist came back. "Someone can be there in just over an hour. They are out on farm calls."

I now understand how this could have happened and how hard it can be to get from one emergency to another. But I had a real emergency, and the next call was to Dad. He happened to be between teaching classes at the high school and picked up the phone.

"Dad, one of the ewes is in trouble. I think the lamb is too big and she is really straining." I was practically yelling into the phone. "The vet can't get here for an hour. What should I do?"

He thought for a moment before answering. "You're going to have to pull it out yourself."

This was not the answer I wanted to hear. One of the last things a fifth-grader can imagine doing is grabbing hold of a lamb covered with fetal fluids.

"Get ahold of the legs and pull hard. You can do it!" he continued.

Not wanting to disappoint my dad, I said I would try and hung up the phone. I ran back to the barn through the wet March grass. Back in the barn, the laboring ewe still lay on her side, panting, while the baby had made no more progress entering the world. I wasn't really up for this, but I was all she had. How could I look at her in pain and not do what I needed to do, even though I was completely grossed out? Taking an especially big breath, I knelt down, gripping the wet, slippery legs, one in each hand. I began to pull the legs toward me and away from mom. The tension on the lamb caused the ewe more pain. She began slamming her head against the barn floor, so I backed off, and she relaxed.

"Easy, girl. I'm sorry," I whispered.

I knew I couldn't continue if it was going to be this painful. I'm sure that some human mothers can relate to this predicament. I decided I was going to have to update Dad. I was hoping that he could come up with something else; maybe he would even come home to fix it himself. So I made another sprint back to the house to use the phone. I guess that he was expecting to hear from me, since he came to the phone, even though he'd been in the middle of teaching a class.

"I can't do it. I'm just making it worse for her when I pull." I didn't try to hide the defeat in my voice.

Then came the calming voice of my father. "You can do this. If you don't get the lamb out, we will lose both of them, but you can do it! Just pull as hard as you can."

"Can't you come home and do it?" I begged.

"I'm sorry, but I can't leave my class," he responded.

I grabbed some clean towels from the bathroom and headed back with renewed determination. This time, I gritted my teeth, grabbed the damp little legs again, and pulled with every muscle in my body. The ewe grunted in pain, but she pushed with her abdominal muscles in an attempt to help me. The little guy moved out about an

inch. Although it wasn't much, both mom and I were encouraged. It was just enough to relieve some of her discomfort. Her breathing slowed down and her general attitude was more relaxed. We both took a one-minute break before trying again. This time, the lamb moved out three inches. I hadn't paid much attention to the physical condition of the baby. He hadn't shown much sign of life, but with this latest thrust, he began to move his tongue a bit. This little sign gave me renewed strength, so I leaned into it one more time. On cue, the ewe, with what little she had left, gave a last push. Like a cork from a champagne bottle, the lamb popped free, ending up in my lap. It was gross to a fifth-grader, but even so, I was able to forget the mess and appreciate the miracle of a new life. My dad had told me that if I got the lamb out alive, I should rub it down to stimulate its breathing. He hadn't said to use my mother's newest towels, but I would deal with that problem later. As I rubbed, he continued to show more signs of life. His tongue kept moving with increased vigor and eventually he worked out a little noise. Although weak and wobbly, he was able get his head up enough to let out a little *baa*. This call brought his ex-hausted mother to her feet. Mothers of all species jump to attention when they hear their newborns cry for them. Even one who appears to be at death's door comes alive when beckoned by her baby. These resurrections are always followed by milk flowing to the right places, producing a first meal for the hungry baby.

The next thing I knew, the lamb had his head under her flank, noisily sucking milk. I rubbed the top of the ewe's head.

"Well, we did it, big girl."

A few minutes before, they had both been on the floor, near death. Now everything was perfect. You can't have anything closer to a miracle than that, especially when you are ten. I left the happy family, exiting the barn and heading back toward the house to let

Dad know. I was practically skipping, feeling nearly invincible. But as is true so many times, when you begin to feel a little too good about yourself, something happens to bring you back down to earth. This day, it was Ben. He had broken a board in his confines, escaping through the hole he'd created. All the commotion from the birth of his new son must have upset him enough that he broke out to see what the deal was. Now there he was, about ten feet in front of me, head lowered and all four legs planted firmly in the mossy spring soil. He wasn't going anywhere, and since I weighed only about half as much as he did, there was no way I was going to win this battle. I so wanted to get to the phone to tell Dad what had happened, but Ben just wasn't going to let me. I don't know if his escape had made him feel especially dominant, but he wasn't going to let me pass without a fight. No matter how invincible I felt at that age, there was no way that I was going to mess with him. Trying to act coy, I slowly turned back toward the open barn door, then sprinted like a deer with a lion on its tail. I slid the heavy door closed behind me with the adrenaline-motivated strength that any scared being can conjure.

Ben slammed his huge head into the barn door just to let me know he was the man and I was not. I would be waiting in the barn now until someone found me. There were worse places to wait than in a barn full of newborn lambs, but I had so wanted to tell someone about what I had accomplished. I wanted it to be known that without me, this birth would not have happened.

Over the next hour and a half, I sat on some extra straw bales, waiting for someone to rescue me. What with the comfortable bales and the warmth produced by the constantly munching sheep, I could easily have fallen asleep if not for all the previous excitement and the fact that Ben would occasionally ram his head into the door just to remind me he was still there.

Finally, I could hear my father in the distance. "Ben, get back in there. Get away from that door."

Ben did respect Dad. He was the only person who could make the big ram do something he didn't want to do. It was probably for the same reasons I did what my Dad said—fear of what might happen if I didn't (which is the way it should be). I could hear Ben stumble back through the boards of the fence to get where he was supposed to be. The barn door slid open and my father's large frame filled up the entry.

"Are you okay?" he asked. "He didn't get you, did he? I can't believe he got out."

"No, I'm fine," I responded, just happy to see him. "But look at the new lamb I pulled."

I told him the whole story, dragging him through every gory detail. He, in turn, listened intently to his ecstatic son relive his first of many experiences with the birth of an animal. He nodded, acknowledging every detail, then slapped me on the back.

"Congratulations. Maybe we've got a veterinarian in the making," he said with a smile. "Now let's fix that fence so Ben stays where he is supposed to."

A couple of nails later, the boards were back in place and we were headed to the house to repeat the whole story again for the rest of the family. I also had to explain the towels.

The oversized lamb grew up quickly, and by the end of the summer, he had made it to the state fair. He showed very well and won a big purple ribbon, which I proudly displayed above his pen. Unwitting fairgoers would come by to look at him and the ribbon he had won, not knowing that I lay in wait to recount the story of how he came into the world.

Not Dog Food

The distinctive shape of a small rubber duck appeared on the abdominal X-rays. The white barium liquid that I had force-fed the poor canine had encompassed the toy duck, revealing its shape. Young dogs will eat almost anything they can get hold of. I have seen them come through the door of the clinic after ingesting anything from rocks to towels, and let's not forget grasshoppers, something I experienced in my early days in practice. In many cases, the family knows what item has been devoured, because it has been missing for a few days. In this case, the little boy whom the pup belonged to had been complaining that he had lost his bathtub ducky. We had a clue ahead of time as to what the culprit was.

As with most pets that have eaten something inappropriate, they tend to present depressed, dehydrating, and vomiting. Since very little food or water gets past the blockage, they rarely can hold anything down. On this day, that "anything" ended up on my shoes as I was examining the patient in the waiting room, taking the expression "foot odor" to a whole new level. He was a young chocolate Lab, so it wasn't just a minute amount. Most of the barium I had gotten down him came back up also, but just enough stayed down to outline the duck and help me narrow down its location in the maze of intestines. Having a reasonable idea of where to look would make it easier for me to extract the object during surgery. The duck had lodged in the small intestine, right outside of the stomach, so very little was making it far enough to be absorbed by the dog. By the time I removed the once-cute yellow rubber duck from the pup's bowel, it was in no shape to be given back to the boy. It was now green and deformed by the strong stomach acids, no longer resembling or smelling like something that a child would want to play with. When the patient's family called to see how the surgery had gone, I suggested they might want to pick up a new duck for their son on the way home, if he was expecting to get it back.

Inappropriate ingestion by dogs will vary by season. One Easter evening, a family brought in their shih tzu after it devoured the largest portion of a life-size chocolate bunny while they were over at grandma's house for dinner. They came home and found their little dog collapsed beside the remains of the holiday treat. When they brought him in for emergency treatment, his heart rate was off the chart. That amount of chocolate, especially dark chocolate, contains enough caffeine to put a small dog into an early grave. It took many bags of fluids to flush him out and a lot of charcoal forced into his digestive tract to absorb the chocolate that hadn't been fully digested yet. After the two treatments and a couple days of hospitalization, the little dog cheated "death by chocolate" and went home to his family. Once settled in, he proceeded to surprise them when the gold foil wrapper that had originally surrounded the bunny was deposited in the middle of the living room floor.

Veterinarians are always amazed at what they end up removing from dogs' intestinal tracts, and some will even make a display of the things that they have extracted in the past.

Cats seem to be way too savvy to throw back things that they should not. In fact, I think, given the chance, they would talk dogs into eating unacceptable items just to see what would happen.

All vets have stories about items that we have removed, but my most memorable one happened during veterinary school and left a permanent scar on my psyche.

It happened during my senior year, while I was on surgery rotation. The three other students and I in the surgery section were presented on a Sunday with a nine-month-old collie who had been vomiting for the last twenty-four hours. It didn't matter to us that it was the weekend, since we were assigned to be at the school pretty much 24/7 at that point. The poor dog's family showed up with their relatively new family pet in our emergency admittance area that afternoon after a thirty-minute car ride from home. They had found that the pup was getting worse when they got home from church, so they headed for the teaching hospital right away. When the canine first got sick, they thought that she had just eaten something that didn't agree with her from the garbage she had knocked over on Saturday morning. Unfortunately, the family was in such a rush because of their concern for Loni that they didn't take the time to change from their church clothes. By the time they got to hospital, none of their clothes was salvageable. A family of four in a small sedan with a vomiting dog is a bad combination.

Dad carried the nauseated Loni into the emergency entrance and we helped him get her back to one of the exam rooms. My fellow students and I carefully placed her on the stainless-steel exam table and proceeded to check her over.

The thing about teaching hospitals, whether human or veterinary, is that there is always an overabundance of students to see every case.

Overly exuberant students are usually waiting to spring on the next case that comes through the door. Their heads are stuffed full of information about diagnostic tests, which they are dying to try out on a real-life case. The patient at a teaching hospital—or in this situation, I should probably say "victim"—needs to be prepared to be poked and prodded in every body orifice, and then some. We were no different, and we swarmed around the dog in an attempt to come up with a diagnosis. After about thirty minutes of not really coming up with anything, we sent the distraught pup down to Radiology to see if anything could be spotted in an X-ray. We sent the family home to clean up and told them we would call when we found something.

One of the many advantages of being at a teaching hospital is that there are many different departments to pass the patient to that have an expert available to help with the diagnosis. Luckily, that day there was a radiologist available, and the students in his rotation were able to call him in.

Dr. Sutherland was a slightly arrogant man to begin with, and when he got called in after hours, he became even more difficult to handle. He was used to being dragged in by students for supposed radiological emergencies that could have easily waited until the next day. He arrived about twenty minutes after having been paged, sporting his dyed hair and gold necklace. Apparently, he didn't want anyone to know that he was actually in his early fifties, especially the female students. But this call obviously wasn't a bogus one. One look at Loni and his attitude changed.

"Get some pictures and see what's going on here," he said as he rubbed poor Loni on the top of her head.

His radiology students scampered off with Loni to the X-ray room to get several shots of Loni's abdomen. When those X-rays were developed, Dr. Sutherland, with his students peering over his shoulder, studied them, contorting his face in dissatisfaction over what he did or didn't see.

"We're going to need to do a barium study," he mumbled. "I can't see anything substantial yet. Hopefully, the barium will show us what we are dealing with."

His students nodded in agreement, which they would have done no matter what he'd said, then disappeared to mix up some barium. A barium study can take a couple of hours in a dog, because the X-rays have to be shot at specific intervals as the barium winds its way through the stomach and then through the intestines.

I gave Loni's family a call to tell them it was going to be a while before we knew anything, but I said I would let them know as soon as we did.

"Please call no matter what time it is. We are really worried about Loni."

I assured them that I would, then joined my classmates in Radiology to wait for the results. It is important to have at least four students waiting on one case in the middle of the night, or at least that is what the powers that be wanted in this hospital. In reality, at that point in our education, it took four heads to make a decision about a case. We were naïve and didn't realize that it would take us a couple of years in practice before we could become decent diagnosticians.

By the time Dr. Sutherland emerged with his followers, it was nearly 5:00 P.M., and besides admitting a few elective surgeries for Monday morning, we had pretty much been in the Radiology waiting room the entire time.

"Well, there is definitely something in there. I can't quite tell where or what it is exactly." He scratched his head. "Just enough of the barium is getting past the blockage that it is hard to pinpoint the precise location, but if I had to guess, I would say it is just outside the stomach, at the beginning of the small intestine."

"What should we do with Loni next?" asked one of my cohorts.

"Get her started on some IV fluids and I will check in on her in a few hours. Don't let her eat or drink anything, either."

I always hated the way the clinicians in school would just bark out some orders and then head home. Yet I always thought it would be kind of fun to have a few students to do that to myself, but I've never been able to pull that off. Anyway, he was right: We needed to get Loni rehydrated before we did anything, especially surgery.

The four of us trotted for Intensive Care, with Loni in tow. At this stage of the game, even placing an intravenous catheter was a major procedure for us. But we got it done, and within an hour life-giving fluids were coursing through Loni's veins, making her a much happier pooch. She was very forgiving, not seeming to hold it against us that we'd had a hard time finding a vein.

We took turns not only calling Loni's family to keep them updated but also caring for Loni while the others got some sleep. The school actually had some rooms for those who had to stay overnight. What we didn't realize at the time was that these experiences were preparing us not only for medical procedures but for dealing with clients and functioning with little sleep.

After a relatively long night, the teaching hospital started to come alive again about seven o'clock on Monday morning. Dr. Sutherland showed up, putting a much livelier and obviously hungry Loni through another round of X-rays.

Afterward, he consulted with Dr. Sterkley, who was in charge of our surgery rotation. He was a stocky, bald man, who, like most surgeons, oozed confidence. He and Dr. Sutherland looked over the X-rays on the viewer while talking in near whispers. They did not want to involve the students when they were not totally sure of their diagnosis. After a little head nodding, the pair turned to us.

"It still appears that the blockage is in the first portion of the small intestines," Dr. Sutherland reconfirmed. "Dr. Sterkley is going to try to remove it with an endoscope."

This was in the early days of endoscopic use in veterinary medicine, so this procedure not only would be less invasive for the patient but also fascinating for us.

The minute the decision was made, the surgery area became a buzz. Our group gathered the appropriate drapes and surgery packs in case the endoscope did not work as planned, and the anesthesia group surrounded Loni to put her under for the surgery. I ran off to call Loni's family to get the okay for the procedure.

"Do whatever you need to do. We all miss her terribly," said the voice on the other end of the phone.

I went on to explain how if we were able to get the blockage out with the scope, Loni's recovery would be a lot shorter. I should have said "If Dr. Sterkley is able to get it out," since endoscopes were so expensive at this point that students were not even allowed to touch them, let alone attempt to operate them.

The scope was connected to a television monitor so that we could all observe the procedure. By the time Loni was anesthetized, the whole surgery suite was filled with students who wanted to observe this relatively new technique. Dr. Sterkley enjoyed all the attention, narrating every step as he slid the instrument down Loni's esophagus and into her stomach.

"Now we have to find the end of the stomach and enter the small intestine. Wells, what is the sphincter called that separates the two regions?" he asked.

Oh crap, I thought. I was so focused on watching the procedure on the monitor that I never thought about being drilled with questions. I had to concentrate. What was it? The last part of the stomach is the pylorus. . . .

"Wells?" He was getting a little grumpy.

"Pyloric sphincter," I choked out.

"It's about time. You may want to bone up on your GI anatomy, Mr. Wells," he responded. When you answered with assurance, he referred to you as "Dr." None of my classmates in the room giggled or snickered; they were just glad they hadn't been asked.

As he moved the end of the scope through the pyloric sphincter into the intestine, his focus swung from me to the mass, which was now in full view.

Even with his face up against the instrument, one could see him raise an eyebrow, indicating he didn't know what he was looking at, either.

"Well, I guess we'll just grab it and see what we've got."

He pushed the tweezer portion out in front of the scope and

grabbed something with it. As he pulled the scope out while keeping the tiny tweezer clamped closed, a piece of clear plastic appeared, about half the size of a sandwich bag. It looked like the kind that was probably part of a microwave package. He slid the scope back in again and came up with more of the same plastic. He kept fishing, bringing out more plastic, a half-dissolved chicken bone, and a couple of small pieces of a lollipop stick. None of these should have caused such a major problem.

Just when it seemed like exploratory surgery was going to be the only option, he grabbed something else. We could see on the monitor that the object didn't want to give when he tugged on it.

Out of frustration, he pulled a little harder, and something gave way. He had to work to drag it back up through the esophagus, but we all knew whatever was about to come out of Loni had to be the cause of the problem. The object clamped to the end of the scope was just a rather nondescript mass of cottonlike material.

Everyone in the room leaned in over Dr. Sterkley to get a closer look, then, just as quickly, recoiled. The cottonlike object was actually a large piece of a feminine product. It had lodged just outside the stomach and swelled. Some of the barium was able to pass through, which was why it was hard to recognize exactly where or what it was in the X-rays. Dr. Sterkley removed the rest of the blockage in several pieces.

Loni recovered from the anesthesia effortlessly and was a happy, bouncy dog almost immediately. The final issue was that one of us from the group had to call the family to let them know how Loni was doing and tell them what we'd found. Fortunately, I had made the last call, letting me off the hook for this one. Since there were three guys and one woman in our group, she was outvoted and reluctantly accepted the task.

The family was elated at the good news. They were just happy to get Loni back safe and sound. Although they did promise that they would empty all the garbage cans before leaving Loni in the house alone again.

Christmas Mule

Just as the Christmas season brings decorations, gifts, and gatherings, without fail it also seems to bring its share of veterinary emergencies. It's almost like the animals get together right after Thanksgiving and decide whose turn it will be this year. I think it must play out like a holiday television special with talking animals.

"Hey, Rex, I think it's you this year. Dr. Wells and his wife have tickets to a Christmas play on the twentieth, so you'd better start working on that hair ball now."

Like most veterinarians, I have treated everything from a new puppy who ate a chocolate Santa to the gift pony who tried to run through the fence on Christmas Eve. This year, the pager buzzed in my pocket at a friend's Christmas party on the twenty-third of December. It was a beautiful get-together. There were cheese, crackers, and wine as far as the eye could see. The guests were getting more and more rosy-faced as the conversation volume increased. As the wine continued to flow, toasts were made, while laughter echoed through the living room and kitchen. Yet for me it had all just come to an abrupt end. I stood frozen in the middle of the living room, glass in hand. The rest of the party continued to go on around me, but I was no longer a part of it. I was about to go back out into the winter night. As always in this scenario, I politely asked the hostess if I could borrow her phone, then called back the client. Cell phones were only starting to get popular and were still too expensive for your average veterinarian.

Mrs. Gerry answered the phone. "Oh, thanks for calling back, Dr. Wells. Pat is out with Molly and she is not doing very well. She is trying to lie on the ground and roll. Pat can hardly keep her up."

I drew a breath, admitted to myself that I would be leaving the party, and said, "I will head that way in just a few minutes. Have Pat keep Molly up and walking until I get there."

Molly was Pat Gerry's pet mule and the second love of his life, after his wife, I think. Pat and his mule rode the mountains almost every weekend. The two of them had covered every trail in our region over the last several years. They were very good buddies, and I knew that Pat would be coming unglued if I didn't get there soon.

Marion and I always attend social events with two cars just because of situations like this one. Too often, I have been called away early, so I always keep my truck within reach. I always store a change of clothes in the truck in order to pull a Superman move when necessary, changing in the truck before I take off into the night. Appropriately, halfway to the Gerrys' it began to snow. Flakes started to build on the windshield and blew into the headlights, making it hard to see the road. I was just able to make out the road sign at the turnoff I was looking for. The Gerrys' house was just a couple driveways from the turnoff, yet I had to concentrate to find it. Enough snow had built up on the mailboxes to cover up the names and addresses. I pulled into what I thought was the right one and my headlights hit the barn in front of me. I recognized the old wooden barn, so I knew I was in the right place. But much to my disappointment, there was no sign of Pat or Molly. I had hoped that we would be able to work on Molly in the shelter of the barn. Continuing down the driveway toward the house, I scanned the woods for the pair, squinting to try to spot them in between the monstrous ponderosa pines. I wasn't having much luck, when they suddenly appeared in front of my headlights. Molly's head hung low and her ears flopped listlessly to the sides of it. They were no longer the upright radar antennas that normally would have honed in on me immediately. Her eyes were half-closed and her back was covered with a thin blanket of snow, adding to her pitiful look.

Pat stood beside her, holding her lead rope in his enormous hand. Pat was a large man, around six four and about a biscuit shy of three hundred pounds. He had a fairly large belly, which stuck out in front of him, and a round, ruddy face. His graying hair was topped with a cap of snow. In his Carhart coveralls, he looked a little like the mountain-man version of Saint Nick himself. I picked up my stethoscope from the passenger seat while sliding out of the truck into the snow.

"Thanks for coming, Doc. She's not doing well at all." His voice cracked a little. "I've been walking her for an hour, but she just wants to lie down and roll. What do you think is going on?"

"Well, let's take a look," I replied as cheerfully as I could. I knew that Molly had colic.

I just wanted to see how bad it was, because I knew that would be Pat's next question. Colic just means that the animal has abdominal pain. In horses, it can be caused by anything from constipation to a twisted intestine. The unfortunate thing for horses and mules is that the construction of their esophagus makes it impossible for them to throw up. Thus it is almost impossible for them to relieve the discomfort on their own. I placed the stethoscope against Molly's side and listened for intestinal movement, hoping to hear the familiar gurgling sounds of a happy intestinal tract, but only an occasional grumble was audible. Even so, a little movement was better than none, giving me some hope for the poor mule.

"She's got some gut sounds," I announced to an anxious Pat. "Let's do a palpation to see if we can tell what's causing all this."

As usual, I meant a rectal palpation, but I often tried to play that part down. Molly felt so poorly that she didn't care what I did and needed no sedation for this procedure. Pat probably could have used some, though. His eyes got pretty wide when I pulled the plastic sleeve up to my shoulder and headed for the business end of the mule. He had not witnessed colic before and was not prepared for what was involved.

"Easy now, big girl," I said, placing my hand on her rump as I slipped my sleeved hand in.

I didn't want to spook her while I was in such a precarious position. Mules are notoriously good kickers, and any other night Molly would have sent me flying.

On this night, however, the procedure was a little less risky. All she wanted was to feel better, and she was pretty much willing to put up with whatever was necessary in order to make that happen. I could feel through the plastic glove that her intestines were filled with gas, which was the source of most of Molly's pain. This amount of intestinal bloating in an equine always makes me extra nervous, because it can indicate a twist in the intestinal tract—a condition that is always severe. Folding my hand to make it as small as possible, I moved farther up the poor animal's insides. The largest risk with this procedure is sticking a finger through the intestinal wall. It is a little too easy to do and usually a fatal error. The resulting hole allows bacteria to escape into parts of the body where they are not supposed to be, producing a raging infection that can easily consume the creature. Thus the slow, easy movement and collapsing of my hand. An intestinal puncture was not an additional problem that Molly needed this evening. As my hand moved over one of the bloated areas, Molly's rear legs gave a bit. The area was obviously sensitive and I had unintentionally caused her pain. Pat winced and shot me a glance.

"I'm sorry, girl. I will try not to let that happen again, but we have got to find the problem," I said as I patted her rump again with my free hand.

"It's okay," Pat whispered while caressing her forehead. "It will be over soon." Then he shot me another icy glance. I hate it when I become the bad guy, but it comes with the territory. At this point, I was finally beginning to take these kinds of looks less personally.

Pat needed someone to be aggravated with right then, so it was going to be me. If that distracted him a little from his concern about Molly, then so be it. "All right, big girl, just a tiny bit farther," I said, encouraging her as I stretched my arm as far as it would go. I had gotten in so far that my shoulder was immersed in fecal matter. But that was fine, because my fingertips could just reach the problem area. A mass of hard, dry feces had managed to get bound up in a spot where the intestines narrow from a larger diameter to a smaller one—not a rare place for an impaction to occur. Molly had probably just not been drinking enough water over the last couple of days and had become a little constipated. I was relieved. A fecal impaction usually held a much better prognosis than a twist. My mood lightened as I eased my hand out of Molly's upset intestines.

"Well, she's got an impaction," I announced to an anxious Pat.

Then came the question that always follows an equine rectal exam: "Is there a twist, Doc?"

"Not that I can find at this time," I replied, then continued with my patented follow-up: "But impactions can lead to a twist, so we are going to have to see how it goes."

Pat nodded solemnly. "What can we do to keep that from happening?"

"Well, we need to treat her aggressively and get the impaction to pass quickly," I said.

Pat gave me another nod, which I interpreted as acceptance and agreement from a man of few words. I set about the task of loosening up Molly's bowels. Molly got an intravenous injection of an anti-inflammatory to relax her constricted intestines, followed by an elephant-size dose of painkiller. The next step was almost as unwelcomed as the rectal exam. I slipped a garden hose–size plastic tube into one of Molly's nostrils, gently easing it down her esophagus and into her stomach. Once the characteristic smell wafted back up through the tube and burned the inside of my nose, I knew we were in the right place. Confident that the end of the tube had ended up in the stomach and not in the lungs, I pumped in a gallon of mineral oil. Then I blew on my end of the tube to be certain all of the thick oil made it out of the tube. This was something I never wanted Marion to witness, due to the fact that fermenting stomach contents might make their way back up the tube before I got it out of my mouth.

"Well, that ought to get things moving," I said to Pat as I pulled the tube back out.

"Yeah, that would do it for me," he replied, his face contorted in disapproval of me and empathy for Molly. I waited for the question I knew was next. "How long do you think it will take before something comes out?"

I thought for a few seconds before responding. The way I answered this one would affect the number of phone calls that I would get from Pat in the next few hours.

"It will probably be several hours. If she is not doing better in three hours, call me back." I practically choked on my own words as I said this, knowing I would be getting a call in three hours. Pat nodded, having had just enough experience with these types of cases to know that Molly was in pretty bad shape and was going to need more treatments. It was reassuring to know that Pat was not going to leave her side. This was his best buddy, and the snow that had buried my truck was not going to hinder his watch. Sliding on my ski gloves, I brushed the snow off my truck and started to get back in the cab, when I heard a throat clear behind me.

"Doc."

"Yes."

"She's in bad shape, isn't she?"

As much as I wanted to be less than honest, I knew that I couldn't pull any punches. "It is a pretty severe blockage, Pat. We are going to have to keep a close eye on her and, as I said before, treat her as aggressively as possible."

I could just make out the big man's Santa-like face through the snowflakes. A couple of tears had frozen to his face just under the crow's-feet at the corners of his eyes. As I backed out of the driveway, he and his still slightly sedated mule faded back into the snow. On calls like this, especially in the middle of a storm, it can seem like the client, the patient, and you are the only people in the world. The highway is empty of cars and the welcoming lights of houses are dimmed by the snow. Even the elk and deer, whose eyes would normally shine by the side of the road, are curled up under the protection of the dense pine trees. No, it was just us tonight and would be again when

I returned in three hours. Walking into the house, I grabbed three extra large bags of IV fluids from the storage closet and placed them in front of the woodstove to warm up. These would probably come in handy in a few hours.

I tossed and turned in bed, knowing I would be back up soon, so when the pager went off at 2:30 A.M., it was no surprise. Marion didn't even have to give me the usual bony elbow. I slid right back into my clothes, grabbed the bags of fluids, and was back in the game. I gave Pat a quick return call to let him know I was on my way there, then blew out the door. The snow had not diminished at all. A couple more inches had built up during my brief attempt at sleep. After wiping off the truck once again, I slid onto the frozen seat and turned the key. The cold engine was as tired as I was. It coughed twice, then quit—not a good sign in the middle of the night, with Pat waiting for me to pull back into his drive. Sitting there in the dark, the snow covering the windshield again, I felt dread in the pit of my stomach. What if the truck wouldn't start? What if I couldn't get anyone to fix it at this time of night? What if Molly died because I couldn't get there in time? My mind was racing as I imagined the worst-possible scenario. I closed my eyes and gave it one more try. The sound of the starter cracked the snowy silence. The engine stuttered twice, then miraculously roared to life.

The trip back seemed to take forever. It always seems to take longer to get to a sick animal than it should, especially in the snow. The highway was snow-packed by this time and mine were the only tracks being made. All the lines had disappeared and I had to lean forward and squint to make out the edge of the road. By the time I pulled into Pat's drive, my head was pounding from eye strain and I was elated just to be off the road. The driveway had filled in with champagne powder that was disturbed only by the tracks of a large man and the distinct ones of a mule. I stepped out of the truck near the barn, hoping we would be able to step inside to examine Molly. I had a feeling I was going to be there for a while and was not overly excited about standing in the snow. The white stuff was about halfway up my calf now and showing no signs of easing. I stood there, eager to examine Molly, but she and Pat were nowhere to be found.

I yelled repeatedly, "Pat. Pat, where are you? I'm down here by the barn." I knew it was futile, but I kept yelling anyway. I had learned that nothing muffled sound better than a Rocky Mountain snowstorm.

A few winters ago, I had been out hiking with a friend, and we managed to get separated for a short time during a snowstorm. Eventually, I was able to see him just up the hill from me, about fifty feet away. I yelled until my throat was sore, yet he couldn't hear me. Finally, I had to hit him with a snowball to get him to notice me.

A while later, a forlorn Santa and his even more miserable-looking steed appeared from the shadows without making a sound. Pat spotted me from under his icicled eyebrows.

"How long have you been here?" he bellowed, gasping for air. "She went down back in the trees 'bout a half hour ago. I just got her up." Molly was soaked from her roll in the snow and began to shiver.

"Let's get her in the barn to work on her," I suggested, and Pat nodded. He had stayed outside with Molly to keep her walking.

Pat slid the door open and, to my surprise, flipped on a light. I hadn't expected electricity, let alone the comfortable straw-covered floor. The place was as clean as a whistle. My evening was looking up. Pat slid the door closed, making it feel as if the storm were miles away.

"Pat, you spoil me," I said, taking in my new surroundings.

"There isn't much room, but there is enough for the three of us," he replied. I happily agreed and began examining Molly. Her wet hair had turned into an icy blanket, making it a little hard to hear what was going on inside, but it couldn't muffle the pounding heart working overtime to pump blood through her weakening body. It was also a clinical sign, indicating the kind of pain caused by severely obstructed bowels.

"Pat, we are going to have to treat her more aggressively or we're going to lose her. We have to get her on some IV fluids to rehydrate her and attempt to get those intestines moving."

"Can we do it right here?" he asked hopefully. We would never be able to get her to a referral center in this storm, and I guessed that he couldn't really afford it anyway.

I nodded. "I've got the fluids in the truck. Let's get started."

I made multiple trips back and forth to the truck. First, I brought more mineral oil to administer through the tube to the stomach, then more painkillers to relax her. Next, I went out to find a catheter and a pair of hair clippers to prepare the area surrounding the jugular vein. I could never remember everything I needed when standing in a blizzard. Pat stood solemnly at his station, rubbing Molly's head and talking quietly to her. Molly didn't feel well enough to care one way or the other, but she kept her head close enough to Pat to receive the unrelenting rubs.

The next step was to get fluids into her. The intravenous catheter is always the most intimidating part of this process, due to the sheer size of it. I always get the same reaction when I pull one out. If you've ever given blood or received fluids yourself, you'll know that a catheter seems more like a pipe being rammed into your arm than a medical device. So you can imagine the reaction when clients see a horse catheter for the first time. Pat did not disappoint me.

"Holy cow, Doc, you're going to put that in Molly's vein? Well, I'm glad it's not going into mine."

Even Molly raised her head a bit and seemed a little astonished. I took Molly's lead rope away from Pat and tied her to one of the barn supports. I found a nail above her head that stuck out just enough for me to hang one of the five-liter bags of fluids on it. I attached the long, skinny IV tubing to the bag, leaving me with only one thing left to do.

Molly's jugular vein was not the easiest to find. The dehydration had made her pulse weak and the vein shrink. Easing the big needle through her tough skin, I probed in a few different directions before the needle found thick, concentrated blood. The plastic cover then threaded easily off the long needle it surrounded and moved deep into the vein itself.

I attached the free end of the IV tubing to the end of the catheter, which was dripping tiny drops of blood. The life-giving fluid flowed freely into Molly's body.

"Now what, Doc?" Pat asked, as if he expected some improvement within seconds.

"Now we wait," I said. "It will take a few of these bags to make an improvement in Molly."

I didn't have the heart to tell him that there would be a lot of cramping and pain on Molly's part before she got better—if she ever got better. Pat seemed a bit disappointed, but he nodded his head. I was just settling down on a hay bale when Pat walked to the door.

"I'll be back in just a few," he uttered before walking back into the storm.

I sat there staring at Molly, her body now a far cry from having the strength it took to haul Pat over mountaintops. I wondered if she would ever be able to do that again.

I had almost drifted off to sleep when the door flew open and Pat stepped back in from the storm. I had no idea how long he had been gone, my only gauge being the first bag of fluids, which was half gone.

"I got us some hot chocolate." Pat lifted a small thermos. "And some carrots for Molly when she feels better."

He raised his other hand to show me the huge bag of carrots. His anticipation of Molly's recovery was refreshing, but what if she didn't make it? There was a good chance of that. I hoped that I hadn't painted too rosy a picture. It would have been easy to do for such a nice guy so close to the holidays. Pat poured from his thermos into one of the Styrofoam cups he had brought with him. A big sip of the hot fluid made me wince. It wasn't just hot chocolate. Pat had been waiting for my reaction. For the first time, he laughed—not a snicker, but a hearty Santa-like laugh.

"A little more in there than you expected, eh, Doc!" He beamed. "I thought I'd better include some peppermint schnapps, it being so close to Christmas and all."

Then he drank down his cup, licked his lips, and sighed. While the rest of the fluid ran into Molly, we sat talking about the times he'd had with her. Pat continued to reminisce while I changed the empty bags to new ones at the rate of one an hour. The time passed quickly as I listened to Pat. He was more talkative than I had ever known him to be. Possibly this was due to the "hot chocolate" he kept sipping. Then about halfway through the third bag of fluids, Molly began to get uncomfortable.

"What's going on, Doc?" Pat asked as he shook off the effects of the "hot chocolate," remembering why we were in this barn.

"She's rehydrated and her intestines are trying to get moving again," I told him.

Knowing what was about to happen, I had an extra syringe of painkiller in my pocket and jabbed it into her vein as she tried to lie down. This time, it didn't give her as much relief as it had previously. The fluids would either make things better or not, and Molly would have to go through some discomfort in the meantime. Pat's face was solemn again.

"You knew this was coming, didn't you, Doc?"

"Yes, it is pretty much up to her now."

We both stood there and stared at Molly. There would be several minute-long periods when she would be relatively pain-free; then a cramp would hit her, nearly dropping her to the floor. I changed the fluid bag again, then sat down on my hay bale to watch it drain. It is a little sad how many nights I have spent waiting for some animal to poop.

The next bag eventually ran out, and I hooked up the last one. I turned down the speed of the drip, knowing we had already reached normal hydration. This last fluid bag would help to sustain her level of hydration and maybe encourage the release that we were looking for.

Peeking out the door of the cozy barn, I found the snow was still falling and our tracks had long disappeared. I would not be curling up in my warm bed again, but at least I had the refuge of the barn. Pat sat down on his bale and I on mine.

"Wait?" Pat looked at me.

I nodded. "All we can do."

He seemed to accept that answer, leaning back against the old wooden wall behind him. Molly appeared comfortable for the most part, only stomping occasionally when the cramping flared up.

"Doc, wake up. You've got to see this! Wake up!" Pat's big paw was shaking my shoulder.

Stiff and dazed from sleeping on a bale of hay in the middle of winter, I struggled to bring myself to life. Light was shining through cracks in the barn walls and a thin lace of snow that had forced its way through the cracks decorated everything inside, including me. But the most noticeable change was the distinctive smell of fresh manure.

"See, Doc," Pat said, pointing a big finger at the single largest pile of feces I had ever seen come out of an animal.

This was worthy of an elephant. Molly gave me a "See what I did" look, then resumed munching on the plethora of carrots that Pat had strewn in front of her. Pat was as happy as a kid on Christmas morning. He was rubbing her head and squeezing her around the neck.

"Thanks, Doc. This was about the best Christmas present I could ever get!" he exclaimed.

I pressed my stethoscope to Molly's side, hearing the rumblings of a now-normal intestinal tract. Her heart rate was back to baseline and her gums were a healthy pink color. It was hard to imagine that relieving a little constipation could be so dramatic. I rubbed her velvety ears, then whispered into them.

"You did good, big girl, but let's not do this again. I don't think Pat and I are up for it." Pat chuckled behind me.

I pulled out the IV and he helped me pack everything up and take it back to the truck. The storm was over, the sun so bright reflecting off the snow that it made both of us squint. Pat thanked me again with a vigorous handshake and I headed for home. The whole world seemed washed clean by the crisp white snow, and it was now morning. I was excited I would be spending Christmas Eve with Marion, especially after this past night. The clinic was closed and it would be a much deserved day off. . . . Then the pager mocked me. It rattled and beeped on the dashboard. I knew I'd better call Marion, as I would not be going home quite yet.

Personality Disorder

Lorraine handed me a note as I walked out of the exam room after having just administered the first set of shots to an adorable litter of six-week-old yellow Labrador puppies. This kind of work always makes you feel a little cruel, because the cute little pups cry and whine. I can't imagine how a pediatrician must feel when he or she has to give multiple injections to an infant.

The note Lorraine gave me said that there was a couple in the waiting room who had dropped in with their twelve-year-old cat. The complaint was a dramatic change in the cat's personality over the last couple of weeks. The Hamiltons had just moved to our mountain community from Texas, and their normally precious kitty had turned into an angry predator that had attacked them in the cab of the rented moving truck.

As soon as the puppies had cleared out, I motioned them into the exam room. The couple placed their plastic carrier, containing the schizophrenic feline, gently onto the exam table and began telling me their story. Mr. Hamilton was a friendly fellow with a big smile, a big belly, and a baseball hat that read RETIRED. His past life appeared to have been filled with an overabundance of southern cuisine, which made it a little hard to breathe at our altitude. The hike from the waiting room was enough to make him huff and puff. Mrs. Hamilton was also cheery with her FAVORITE GRANDMA T-shirt and short gray perm. She, too, may have favored fried food, but this just added to her jolly demeanor.

I introduced myself and followed this with the usual question: "What seems to be the problem?"

"Fabio has always been the sweetest thing. He found us years ago when he showed up on our doorstep, but this week he has gone a little loco. Every time we tried to touch him, he would take a swat at us," said Mrs. Hamilton, "He even bit me so badly that I had to see a doctor along the way. He had the audacity to suggest that we find our precious Fabio a new home. Can you believe the gall of that man?"

Several times over the years, owners had brought in their oddly acting cats, only to have me inform them that their multiple-personality kitty was just in heat. Since this cat was a he, I could take that one off my differential diagnosis list.

Mr. Hamilton cautiously opened the door to Fabio's carrier and inched his hands in. A low growl caused him to hesitate for a second, but he closed his eyes and proceeded onward. After a fair amount of hissing from within, Mr. Hamilton produced a very perturbed cat from its confines, placing it in the middle of the table. Now Mr. Hamilton was really breathing heavily.

I quickly lifted the animal's tail to double-check, and sure enough, neutered male. The Hamiltons stared at me across the table, waiting to see how looking in that area was going to help me find the problem.

I performed the rest of the exam while my mind was racing through the possible diagnoses for felines gone mental; then I noticed the scratch marks near the base of Fabio's ears. They were a little hard to make out under his long white hair, but with the hair pulled back, the clue was revealed. Thank goodness I had found something to hang my hat on.

"Did you happen to notice these marks around his ears?" I pointed the scratch wounds out to the Hamiltons. "This could be a clue to our problem."

I touched the left ear gently, right where it attached to the head. Fabio mustered another low growl, letting me know that was the spot. When I repeated the same move on the right ear, he hissed, as if to say, Didn't you think this one would hurt, too?

"I believe we had better sedate him a little and take a good look in those ears," I informed the Hamiltons. They nodded and I pulled up the appropriate medications to give Fabio a short nap. I waved Christie into the room to hold him while I administered the injection into his thigh. Usually, the shot would cause a cat to put up a little bit of a fight, but whatever was going on in Fabio ears was much more painful than the injection.

The Hamiltons and I made light conversation while Fabio drifted off. "We're moving from Texas to escape the heat and bugs," Mr. Hamilton continued. "We have always wanted to live here, and now that we have retired, we just did it. I just hope that Fabio can adjust to his new environment."

I hoped that Mr. Hamilton would be able to adjust.

They seemed so happy to be here that I didn't have the heart to bring up the fact that even though it never got extremely hot here, we often received three to four feet of snow in one storm. Extreme snowstorms were always a little shock for displaced Texans.

Within a few minutes, Fabio had fallen asleep. I dug the otoscope out of the drawer in the exam table and attached the appropriate-size plastic cone to fit inside Fabio's ears. Thanks to the anesthetic, he didn't move at all as I slid the cone down into his ear canal. I flipped on the otoscope's light and looked in, expecting to see the blood-tinged fluid typical of a raging ear infection. The sides of the canal were red and irritated, but there were none of the signs of infection. I slid the instrument deeper into the ear in search of the elusive eardrum. I couldn't seem to see it, even though I knew the scope was in the right place. The view was obscured by a brownish substance that took up all the space between the end of the plastic cone and the missing eardrum.

While squinting my right eye into the scope, hoping to see something more definite, I tried to explain the situation to the Hamiltons. "Well, there seems to be a substance blocking the canal. . . ."

At that moment, something moved in my field of view, or at least I thought that it did. Okay, my eye must be getting exhausted from staring into the tiny hole, I thought. I squinted even harder, hoping to see some other clue. Sure enough, something seemed to run right through my view.

"What in the . . ."

Then it hit me: The entire brown blockage was moving, heaving like the alien nest in a science-fiction movie. It was definitely alive. In the real world, the mass could only be one of two things, mites or ticks.

"I think we need to do some flushing. We may have found the source of Fabio's personality change."

The Hamiltons looked a little puzzled. "So you don't think we need an animal communicator?" Mrs. Hamilton inquired. She went on to explain that they'd decided if this visit didn't help, a communicator would be the next step. She continued: "Some of my friends have used them and swear by their results."

"No, I don't think that will be necessary," I replied while reaching into the drawer for a bottle of ear flush. It was hard for me to imagine Fabio on a couch, explaining to someone how parasites in his ears were making him nuts.

I filled the ear with enough of the blue liquid to drown any little aliens living inside. The three of us leaned over the sleeping cat, staring at the ear to see what would appear. Then a tick floated to the surface, all eight legs treading ear flush. Ticks, Texas size. Others immediately began crawling out, more quickly than I could collect them. I crushed them in a paper towel to make sure they wouldn't infect any other animals in the clinic, including myself.

The Hamiltons reacted by contorting their faces in disgust and unconsciously rubbing their ears as they watched the ticks abandon ship. I flushed a few more times and checked for holdouts with the scope.

"Looks like we got them all," I announced. "I counted twelve. Now let's see how many we get out of the other ear."

"Other ear?" Mr. Hamilton seemed appalled.

Apparently, the thought of the opposite ear having the same infestation had never crossed his mind. Flipping Fabio to his opposite side and filling that ear produced the same results. Only ten escaped from this one.

The best part was the knowledge that the cat would feel relief immediately. Not very often do we veterinarians get to help give an animal such quick resolution.

When Fabio woke up, even his eyes looked better. They were calmer and less terrorized. Christie handed Fabio back to Mrs. Hamilton and he purred calmly, nestling into her arms.

"Oh, I've got my little Fabio back. He's not angry anymore," she cooed.

"Thank you for your help, Doc," Mr. Hamilton said in his Texas drawl. "You have given me back my happy home. Now we can move into our new house without fear of being attacked." All the Hamiltons left the clinic that day in a much better frame of mind.

They brought Fabio in for a recheck about a week later and he let me look in his ears without the help of any chemical restraint. The ears looked great, back to normal and no new creatures in them.

"Fabio has been acting totally normal since our last visit," said

Mrs. Hamilton. "We can't thank you enough for giving us our baby back. I just don't know what we would have done if you hadn't gotten those nasty little creatures out."

Fabio never looked back. Colorado mountain ticks tend not to be quite as abundant or aggressive as the Texas ones and never found their way into his ears. Yet I always wonder how different the results might have been if the communicator had gotten the chance to talk them out.

Stay Off the Internet

D oc, I think I need you to come out and put Peanut down." This was the first call that I picked up on a wet spring morning. Lorraine had handed me the phone just after eight o'clock. She made a grimace, whispering, "It doesn't sound too good." Mrs. Nelson had called in concerning her family's horse. They had found Peanut that morning standing out in the spring snow, surrounded by blood.

He had evidently gotten caught in the fence during the night and, as Mrs. Nelson stated next, "had cut himself horribly." She continued: "I don't think there is any way to save him. Can you come out right away?"

"I'll move some appointments around and get out there." Lorraine rearranged the morning appointments while I made sure that I had enough euthanasia solution for Peanut.

Driving to emergencies like this one is always a tad stressful. I dread what I am going to find and I always wish that I could get there faster. Once I tried to talk the local sheriff's department into giving me a flashing light for the top of my truck, but they weren't really up for it. Instead, they did cut me some slack when I would fly by them as they were trying to catch speeders. They would usually flash the lights atop their squad cars as my truck whisked by, letting me know that they'd seen me speeding but were allowing me to go this time in case it was urgent. I would give the officer an acknowledging wave and speed on.

Peanut lived on the top of a ridge in a field with a view of Pikes Peak that most humans would love to have. The view was great, but the road to get there was winding. I had to manage through four switchbacks to get to the Nelsons'. After driving past a collection of reclusive cabins tucked in behind the lodgepole pine, I finally crested the ridge, and the dense forest opened, exposing the Nelsons' spread before me. The large wood-frame house stood majestically on the spot where the best view could be found, with Peanut's one-stall barn only about fifty feet off to one side.

Mrs. Nelson ran to greet me as I drove toward the barn. "No no! He's not in the barn. Let me jump in with you and I will take you to him."

She was out of breath from exercise combined with panic. I grabbed the usual paperwork and candy wrappers that I stored on the passenger seat, stuffing them onto the dash in front of me.

Mrs. Nelson jumped in and continued after refueling with oxygen. "I left him right where I found him, standing right next to the fence where he tore himself up. Doc, it's not easy to look at."

Preparing myself, I turned downhill in the direction that she was pointing and followed the fence line. I could make out Peanut's form in the distance. He was completely white, with dark black hooves. I knew that his long white winter coat would be drenched in blood, and blood always looks worse on white. Snow doesn't help, either.

As we pulled up next to Peanut, none of the scenarios that I had created in my mind was present. He was standing quietly, munching hay that someone had put there to keep him still. There were only a few drops of blood in the snow and his glistening white leg was marred by just three or four stripes of red running from the wound to his hoof. The laceration itself was covered by a four-inch piece of gauze affixed to Peanut's hair with white medical tape. I was a little confused that the wound that had been described would fit under a four-inch piece of gauze.

"So, have you moved Peanut from where he was originally injured?" I asked.

"No. This is right where we found him," she replied. "Isn't it awful?" The tape pulled on Peanut's hair as I peeled off the bandage, causing him to dance a little. The tear was about one inch long and about half an inch wide.

"I know it's not good, Doc. I researched horse cuts on the Internet before I called you. I know that cuts like this can often cause horses to bleed to death or kill them by infection." Now the puzzle came together: The Internet was involved. Although the World Wide Web is an unbelievable source of invaluable information, I have found that some sources seem to exaggerate veterinary issues, inducing panic in clients. "It said that if I could see muscle under the cut that it was bad and could easily become infected. Do you think you can actually fix it?"

"Peanut is going to be fine," I replied confidently. "We just need to clean the wound up and put a few sutures in."

"Are you sure? You know, it said on the Internet . . ."

"I know, but trust me, he'll be fine," I said.

I tried again to convince her. This time, she seemed to be resigned to the fact that Peanut didn't face certain death. The wrinkles in her

forehead started to ease and I thought even the corners of her mouth may have turned up a little. She held on to Peanut while I collected the necessary items from my truck. I then clipped the white hairs away from the wound. Sometimes getting the hair out of the way will make a cut appear larger, but not even a shave could exaggerate this one. It was just plain small. After I cleansed the entire area with antiseptic, it was time to inject lidocaine around the wound so that Peanut wouldn't feel anything when I sutured it closed. Peanut had been more than a good patient during the whole procedure, but even he was going to need a bit of sedative before I blocked the wound. When I brought out the needle to pull up the sedative, Peanut's eyelids sprang open. I stroked the side of his face and said, "Just one little poke and everything after will be a blur."

"You know," Mrs. Nelson chimed in, "the article on the Internet warned about sedating horses that have suffered significant blood loss. It said that this would lower their blood pressure too much and they could die."

I acknowledged her comment as I found Peanut's vein and injected the drug. "They are correct. The sedation can be very hard on animals that have lost significant amounts of blood, but Peanut should be fine." She seemed happier that I had acknowledged that the Internet had some merit in situations like these and let me go on with my job. Peanut's eyes soon glazed over and he eased into the stupor I had been looking for.

Everything was going nicely as I put the first two sutures in. The wound was beginning to close, and Mrs. Nelson bent over to observe my handiwork.

Her head was only a few inches from mine by the time she said, "Yep, that looks like the way they did it on the Internet."

I had about had it with the Internet comparisons, when I noticed Peanut wobbling just a little more than he should. Mrs. Nelson noticed, too, and backed herself away. I stood up, acting as if I was just stretching out my back. I did need to stretch, but I also wanted to observe Peanut for a minute.

"He seems a little wobbly, don't you think, Doc?" I didn't answer right away, assuming this had also been described on the Internet. He seemed to be getting progressively worse, almost buckling at the knees. "Well . . ." I began to try to answer her, when Peanut simply lay down.

Now by this time in my career, I had sedated hundreds of horses. I knew that I had given Peanut the correct dosage and I was sure that he hadn't lost enough blood to have caused a problem with the sedative, but how had this happened? Mrs. Nelson didn't seem astonished at all. In fact, she just stood there unfazed. I, on the other hand, nearly panicked. His gums were still pink, indicating that it was not blood loss. Grabbing my stethoscope, I listened to his heart and lungs. His heart rate and breathing had both slowed. He was also sweating profusely. It had to be the sedative. I had heard of horses having trouble with it once in a great while, but I had never seen it happen. As we say in veterinary circles, "If it can happen, it will happen," and this was one of those times.

Luckily, there was a reversal agent for the sedative and there happened to be some in my truck. Tearing through my supplies, I found the tiny bottle, which was a little out-of-date, but I thought it should still work fine. I pulled up a slug of it and jabbed it into Peanut's vein.

"Is that the reversal?" Mrs. Nelson asked knowledgeably.

"Why, yes," I replied, not having the time to ask right then how she knew that.

After the reversal, I knew that it would take about fifteen to twenty minutes before Peanut came back to life, or at least that was what the bottle said. The label was a little hard to read, since it was one of those medications that one rarely uses and it had banged around in the truck in the meantime. It looked like one of those old pharmacy bottles that you might see in a museum.

Taking advantage of the recovery time, I put the rest of the sutures in Peanut's skin. It took only three more, bringing the grand total to five. Not much to write home about, but at least Peanut was starting to show signs of life. His respiratory rate was beginning to pick up and the sweat was beginning to dry.

Patting him on the shoulder, I whispered, "Okay, big guy, you really need to get up now. I don't want to lose you, and you're making me look bad." After getting to my feet, I tugged on his lead rope and he hopped right up. I had lucked out this time.

I put together some antibiotic powder for Peanut and handed it to Mrs. Nelson. Then I had to ask, "Weren't you concerned when Peanut went down?"

She looked a little puzzled, then said, "The Internet said that might happen."

Then There Were Three

Marion and I had been parents to many pets of many species. We raised them, loved them, disciplined them, exercised them, brushed them, hugged them, moved them, tended to them, and said good-bye to some of them. There had been five horses, two mules, three dogs, and six cats that made up our family over the years since our marriage. It was natural. Even some of my clients' animals were like family. Julio, our neighbor's miniature donkey stud, brayed at me every morning. Pepper, one of the dude-ranch dogs, would always accompany me as I walked to a corral to tend to a horse, day or night, hot or cold. The Wilsons' barn cat would greet me as she awoke from a sunny spot in the driveway whenever I came to call. However, no amount of scooping horse poop, cleaning litter boxes, or picking up after dogs (even large dogs) could have prepared us for what lay in store once we'd decided, after ten years of marriage, that we were ready to adopt a human child.

Adoption is not one of those decisions made without a lot of thought and love. There is no "Oops" associated with adopting a child. Parents who adopt tend to be very serious about it; otherwise, they would not survive the rather long, painstaking process. On a blistery Rocky Mountain New Year's Eve, we signed the paperwork to get the process started.

Clients of mine had a wonderful daughter whom they had adopted through a Denver-area agency, and they had connected us with the appropriate people. Their little girl was from South Korea and they had been nothing but happy with the whole process. So that New Year's Eve, we signed on to adopt a baby girl from South Korea. The problem is that once you've made the decision and signed on the dotted line, you are ready to have your baby show up, but that is not really the way it works.

In broken English, the Korean lady who ran the agency explained the process: "It will be little over year and half before you baby will come. You now number fifty-six on list for Korean girl with our agency." She continued: "You will be assigned social worker who will visit your house three time before baby comes to be sure that you are appropriate parents in stable situation."

We also would be fingerprinted within an inch of our lives and required to take parenting classes. My first reaction was that if pregnant teenagers don't have to meet these requirements, why should I at forty-three? Marion calmed me down, reminding me of one of my favorite movie quotes. "You have to have a license to own a dog, but anyone can have a kid." Okay, maybe it was a good idea to have some preparation.

Over the next several months, we met our social worker, who turned out to be great. She made the official three visits to our house, which were uneventful except for when she meet our Akita, Beau, and momentarily mistook him for a bear. At 130 pounds, he was an impressive sight. Once she got to know him, she realized that he was not a problem and thus would not put "bear in house" on her report.

After almost a year, we managed to get over all the hurdles. Even the parenting classes turned out to be a good thing. We learned a lot about Korean culture and sampled a variety of Korean cuisine. We both left with the knowledge that kimchi was never going to be a big part of our diet. With this checked off our list, there was nothing left to do but wait, and wait we did.

The next New Year's Eve came and went without any word, and the following months crept by. There were periods when we thought it just wasn't going to happen. We even toyed with looking into another agency. Just when we thought we had reached the end of our rope, the phone call came at the end of April. We were at the top of the list and a baby girl had been born at the adoption-agency home in Korea.

Marion called from work. "Check our e-mail; they've sent us pictures." They were pictures of the most beautiful little girl I had ever seen. She was so tiny and precious, and she was coming to live with us!

Now, if anyone believes that an expectant woman has to be pregnant to exhibit hormonal nesting behaviors, you would be wrong. The photos of our soon-to-be daughter set off a barrage of baby shopping. Fortunately, babies grow up before they wear out their strollers and bedroom furniture; thus our porch became a depository for used baby accessories. There was a stroller for walking, one for running, and even one with heavy-duty tires and suspension for rough terrain. I was being introduced to a multimillion-dollar business that I hadn't realized existed—baby stuff.

The second wave of items was furniture—a baby changer and huge crib that I would have been more than comfortable in. The last item for the baby's room was the most baffling, yet it turned out to be the most valuable—the Diaper Genie. To my disappointment, it was not an ornate bottle that, when rubbed, produced a beautiful young woman who wanted to grant me three wishes or even take dirty diapers off my hands. This genie's bottle was about ten inches in diameter, two feet tall, and made of hard white plastic. The inside of this cylinder was lined with a disposable perfume-infused plastic bag and topped with a twistable lid, so it did have some magical traits. A friend of mine who had been through the birth of two young boys was kind enough to demonstrate how it worked. "You just shove the stinky used diaper inside the cylinder, shut the lid, and twist." He smiled at me, realizing my innocence when it came to the toxic waste I was about to deal with. "The diapers won't smell up the room this way. Just change the bag when it gets full." What he didn't tell me was how often that would be.

We stood in front of the house, looking at all the generous drop-offs and wondering where we were going to put it all. The little room that we had planned to use as a nursery would barely hold the new crib, let alone the changer and genie. We turned to each other at the same time and said, "We're going to have to build on." I contacted a contractor and we started the nursery addition within two weeks. Based on the original date that we had been given for our daughter to arrive, the construction should be done just in time, but as luck would have it, even adoptions don't always go as scheduled.

Just as the molds went up for the new concrete foundation, we received a call from the adoption agency. The message was relayed to us by one of the receptionists. She said that the manager had called and just said, "Wells baby come early." We did not really know what to think of that, and neither did the receptionist. The next day was Friday, on which we received another call, saying that our baby would arrive on the following Tuesday. We were to be at the airport at 6:00 P.M. to pick her up. Women from the agency in Korea would fly with her as far as California and then a retired airline employee from Colorado would pick her up there and take her back to the airport in Denver. The new reality was that the nursery could never be finished by then without a real genie, so all the furniture was going into our bedroom for now. After an insane weekend of preparing, we were as ready as we were going to be for the arrival of our little princess.

The anticipation was nearly overwhelming as we made our way to the airport late that afternoon, and I said a quick prayer that everything would go well. Waiting for us there was a small herd of friends and relatives who had gathered for moral support. Fortunately, Marion had gotten me out of the clothes I'd worn for work that morning, dressing me in a nice white button-down shirt and new jeans so as not to embarrass her in front of her friends and family.

It was great for everyone to be there, but it didn't make the expectant father any less nervous. I paced up and down in front of the escalators where the arriving passengers would come into the main terminal. Day-to-day veterinary practice had made me into a rather cool character in times of stress and anticipation. How many foals had I pulled in a cold barn? How many bleeders had I cauterized on the swollen veins during a tough dog spay? Yet right then, I was completely scattered.

There was another couple awaiting the arrival of their baby girl from the same agency. They already had adopted a child from South Korea, so this was to be their second. They were so calm and I was so not. Attempting to settle my nerves, I joked with the expectant parents and tried to make light conversation. But everything that came out of my mouth was all wrong. I sounded like a babbling idiot. One of our friends even kicked me from behind to get me to shut up. Eventually, the couple excused themselves politely and retreated to another corner of the airport.

Dozens of people poured off the escalators. Travelers came and went, but there was no sign of our precious cargo. I chatted with our support crew and made light of my lack of parental experience. I joked about bottle-feeding puppies and how this would be no trick, but little did I know.

Marion appeared much calmer than I, laughing with our friends while watching out of the corner of her eye as people came in off the arriving planes. But I knew the waiting was killing her. The time had long passed since our daughter's plane was to have landed. They would surely be coming into view soon. We stood beside each other now, out in front of our friends so that we could be the first to see what we were waiting for. I held Marion's hand, then let it drop. As the escalators descended, a small woman carrying a tiny infant approached us with a huge smile. The delivery women must have been given pictures of the anxious couple ahead of time, or she could just guess by the looks on our faces.

Jin, the most beautiful, perfect girl in the whole world, still in her special traveling clothes from a very faraway place, was handed to us. Marion was speechless. She cried silently. I don't think she took a breath for at least five minutes. In an instant, I watched my wife become a mother. Now the gates opened and the tears flowed. There was no holding back. She kissed the little girl repeatedly on the checks and forehead, not missing a single spot. She then squeezed the baby to her chest as if she would never let her go. The dynamics of the group were not unlike those of a group of curious mares in a field with a newborn foal. All the women wanted to see the new baby and nuzzle it. The stallion, or in this case, husband, just stands still if he knows what is good for him.

When Marion finally got Jin back, she handed our daughter over to me and I placed her on my shoulder. My world stopped. I was unaware of the throngs of people around me who had stopped on their way to the baggage claim just to watch the event unfold. Jin was tiny, warm, and quiet. She was curious, yet not afraid.

She settled into my arms, looking up at me with trusting eyes, as if to say, It's about time you guys showed up. Now let's get this show on the road.

We learned from the lovely lady who delivered Jin to us about what she'd eaten on the plane, how much she slept, and how much Korean formula to give her. We took pictures, passed Jin around one more time to our friends and family, and slowly the group got smaller and smaller. Then it was just the three of us—our family, not including the furry ones we couldn't bring to the airport.

Luckily, Jin arrived in July, so we didn't have to battle blizzards on our way back up into the foothills. Jin fell asleep in her brand-new car seat just as we pulled away from the airport. It had been a long day for such a wee tot, and she didn't make a peep. Marion and I were just starting to feel like this whole parenting thing wasn't such a big deal, until we pulled into the driveway. Stopping the car was the green light for Jin to wake up and move directly into screaming mode. We hustled her into the house, still in her car seat. Jin was only three and a half months old, so she was an easy tote.

Inside the house, Beau sat upright from his nap. We had tried to ready him by exposing him to baby clothes, toys, and friends' kids—all the tricks that people had told us would prepare him for this day. He had been sort of an only child up to this point. Yes, he had to share us with a couple of cats and horses, but he had never considered them real competition. For the last six years, he had made the house his domain, but from this moment on, things would never really be the same for him. He gave a furtive glance at his mommy, and Marion quickly reassured him. Our plan was to give him as much attention as possible, so he wouldn't feel he was going to be left out.

"Good boy, Beau. It's going to be fine," we both said as we rubbed his head and kissed his nose.

We could tell that he wasn't buying what we were selling. He followed on our heels as we walked around the house, trying to see what was producing all the racket. We let him sniff and check out Jin for a moment. I am still not sure which one of them was more surprised to see the other up close, but the screaming just increased, and Beau began to look more and more perplexed. Who was this tiny little human who had invaded his lair, why was she making so much noise, and when was she going to leave?

A hard knock on the door shook us out of our introductions. Our neighbor Bobbi, mother of Julio the donkey and two grown boys, marched in with huge bags of baby items under each arm. She scooped Jin up, walked us through the formula procedure, and settled Jin right down. By the time she left, she had given us some invaluable advice. She said to leave a few milliliters of formula in the bottle as we placed Jin down, so she could put herself to sleep before we removed the bottle.

The house was finally quiet, our brand-new family member was asleep, and all of us, including Beau, could relax. Beau usually slept in our room at the top of the stairs, but with the baby now there as well, he slept downstairs—under protest.

Marion and I curled up in our bed beside the crib after checking to be sure Jin was breathing fifteen times. The anticipation and excitement of the day had been too much. We were completely exhausted.

Just before we drifted off, Marion cuddled in next to me and whispered, "I'm so glad you will be here with me all day tomorrow."

This statement got me sitting straight back up. Here, all day! I had set up a full day of appointments. I'd just thought that since Marion wasn't going to be recovering from a delivery or cesarean section, I could . . . I would need to call Lorraine first thing in the morning and postpone as many of those appointments as possible.

I laid my head back on the pillow, hoping not too many people would be upset with me. After what seemed like only a couple seconds of sleep, the tiny body next to us in the crib began to stir, initiating me into the rites of what would be countless middle-of-the-night feedings.

At the crack of dawn, I dragged myself to the phone and called Lorraine at home. After I explained the situation, she said, "Well, what were you thinking, setting up those appointments right after your new baby arrived? I'll get most of them put off, but you will have to go out to the McCallisters'. Their horse is very lame." I was too tired to say anything before she hung up, but why had she let me set up all those appointments if she knew it was going to be a problem?

We spent most of that day playing with and feeding our precious little girl. Talk about frequent meals! There was no rest for the weary. Having put off the McCallisters as long as I could, I headed out to their place a little after 4:00 P.M. They stood in the drive, holding their horse and looking very displeased. I apologized profusely, but I was just too tired to go into the whole reason I was so tardy. They had a friend visiting from out of town, who came out to get in on my examination. She was a friendly soul, about fifty years old, with short, dark hair and a big smile.

"Weren't you at the airport last night picking up a baby?" she asked.

I nodded, eyes half-open.

She went on to explain that she had been one of those who had stopped to observe Jin's debut.

She teared up a little when describing to the McCallisters what a beautiful thing it had been to watch. She told them about how the lady had come in off the plane and put the baby in my wife's arms.

Immediately, I was forgiven for being late. I think the McCallisters were even wiping their eyes a bit.

Over the next few months, Beau started to accept that the little creature, who was now crawling well enough to invade his space, wasn't leaving. He seemed to be somewhat fascinated by her attempts

to crawl across the kitchen floor, and he even gave her a few licks on the cheek when she cried after landing facedown.

All the signs in their growing relationship looked positive, but one particular incident that following winter sealed it for me. We had been having some trouble with a leak from one of our sinks and had called the plumber to repair it. He'd had a busy day, so he didn't show up until right before supper. He was a nice guy, someone I had known for years. He had dogs of his own and was a big dog lover. Jin was in the high chair, with Beau in his usual position on the floor beside her, just in case any crumbs happened to come his way—a symbiotic relationship that probably helped with their bonding process. The plumber bent over to say hi to the two of them and triggered a response that I hadn't expected.

Beau curled his lips and let out a growl that would have frightened the devil himself. Having never seen Beau show any sign of aggression before, I was totally caught off guard. The plumber must have jumped back five feet.

"Beau! It's okay," I yelled. But he had already gotten his point across and just sat up beside the high chair in a guardian pose. For a minute, I wondered if he was even going to let me near Jin.

I apologized to the plumber as he made for the door, nearly leaving his coat behind.

"I understand. He was just protecting the baby. It was stupid of me," he said, still looking a little pale as I handed him a check for his services. It was a good thing he had fixed the sink first, because there was no way he was coming back.

Beau had found his new job as Jin's keeper. We just needed to work on his approach a little.

You Want Me to Do What?

Y ou want me to do what? But it's one A.M."

I was returning the call from Mr. Usher that had induced my pager to rip me from a dream, one whose ending I would never know now. Instead of enjoying the atmosphere of serenity I had been in, I was now completely disoriented. Marion just pulled the covers over her head. She was used to the sound and knew she was not the one who might have to go out into the night. Most of the time, I was not nearly this grumpy, but it was way too early to start my day.

Mr. Usher was a rather wealthy client. I had done a government-regulated blood test on his daughter's horse so that she could join the horse-jumping show circuit in New York State for the summer. Now the horse transport had showed up at their house, but Mr. Usher had forgotten to come by the clinic to pick up the test-result paperwork, which was required if the horse was to cross state lines. They would not be able to transport the horse without the paperwork. He was asking—well, more like demanding—that I meet him at the clinic so that he could get it, and he didn't seem to care about the time.

I tried to convince him that it really wasn't my problem that the transport had showed up in the middle of the night. There had been ample time for him to pick up the test results the day before, but he wasn't having any of it.

"All right, I'll be there in twenty." I was too tired to argue more, and it wasn't worth the repercussions.

I was back home in bed by two o'clock, but I just couldn't get back to dreamland. The aggravation had ruined it for me, and by six the second call of the morning came in. I was off.

As you venture into the stage of what would be considered "an experienced veterinarian," you begin to feel as if there are not as many new situations that can throw you off. There are fewer illnesses that you haven't seen before, less time spent fretting over what to do next, and less heartfelt terror when the receptionist hangs up the phone, only to announce that a dog who was hit by a car is coming in the door. But though these cases were not as apt to throw me these days, the circumstances that surrounded them were still never simple.

The six o'clock call came from a local rancher. "I've got a cow with a prolapse. When can you be here?"

A prolapsed uterus was always a tough case to deal with, even though I had had to do so more times that I wanted to remember. It meant that the animal had most likely had a baby but had had a rough time bringing it into the world. As a result, the uterus had slipped out of the body, following the offspring into the light of day. Obviously, it couldn't stay this way. It needed to go back into the mother the same way it had come out. It might seem like you could just shove it back in and be on your way, but there are extraneous factors. The main one is that the uterus begins to swell the minute it flops out of the body. This occurs because the fluid flowing into it is not able to be reabsorbed back into the mother, due to some blood vessels becoming compromised when the uterus moved outside. Getting the uterus to return to a more normal size was the reason why I would be stopping by the grocery store to pick up some sugar before reaching my patient.

Sugar has been the key to replacing a misplaced uterus since the earliest days of veterinary medicine. Spread thickly over the exposed surface, the sugar pulls out some of the excess fluid, literally shrinking the uterus to a much closer to normal size before your eyes.

The rancher, a scrappy little character with dark hair and even darker eyes, was impressed. "Well, it ought to be easy now, Doc; it's nearly half the size it was." Mr. Sykes was nearly dancing a jig as he watched the uterus diminish as it lay on the lush spring grass behind the cow. She was down on her side, with no interest in getting up. Her new calf was in the house, getting warm and taking its first meal via a bottle. I knew Mr. Sykes was thinking that I wouldn't charge as much now, since the job looked like it was getting easier. He was the type of client who wouldn't think of calling before an animal was in really bad shape.

"Otherwise, it just might get better on its own," I once overheard him tell another client.

After a good dose of sugar, the exposed uterus was a bit less intimidating, but resolving the problem still involved squeezing something the size of a beanbag chair back into the cow through an opening the size of a coffee can. The job involved a lot of groaning, shoving, and even a few quiet expletives on my part. As far as the cow went, she was completely oblivious, since I had slipped her a numbing epidural and she couldn't feel a thing in that area.

The added trick to this already-overwhelming task was being especially careful not to tear or puncture the uterus with a finger. This type of damage would greatly decrease the cow's chances of survival. The palms of the hands and the front of one's chest tend to be the best tools for uterus replacement. It seems that these cases always end in a similar fashion. Just when I am completely exhausted, thinking that this one is going to get the best of me, the defiant organ gives in, disappearing back into the cow. This time was no different.

The only thing left to do was to put in a few sutures so that this condition would not reccur right away. It would only take a few minutes, and then I would be down the road for my next appointment. Gathering the necessary instruments, I placed the first ligature and began to close just enough area to keep the uterus from coming back out. I had only about three more to go, when the cow decided she was done. Evidently, she felt much better after becoming whole again and got up to look for her calf. The epidural that I had given her before attempting the procedure had begun to wear off, and before I could finish, she was wobbling off, with me following behind, holding the suture. Her speed was impaired by her instability, so I was able to keep up at just under a run. Mr. Sykes's laughter was a little distracting, but I finished the last stitch at approximately one hundred yards from the starting spot. The only thing that got me to the finish was the thought of having to replay the whole procedure if I didn't finish the job.

After a couple more ranch calls that morning, I got to the clinic around noon to conduct small-animal appointments. Running behind, I blew into the clinic, hoping to avoid Christie's glare. She hated it when I was late, as the clients tended to take it out on her. I went in the back door so that no one could see me from the waiting room, then pulled off my blood-soaked coveralls. The door from the waiting room cracked and a scowling Christie slid in, closing the door behind her.

"Where have you been? The natives are getting restless."

"Well, I had to go to . . ." I started to explain, but she would have none of it.

"Whatever. I've heard it all before. I've got a dog named Toddles in here with a bloody nose, and a vaccination waiting after that. I already put the bloody nose in the exam room, so it won't make such a mess in the waiting area."

That made sense, so I slipped into my light blue lab coat and went on in to take a look. On the Formica table sat a happy standard poodle with blood dripping slowly from his nostrils. With him was a teenage girl, probably in her late high school years, and her boyfriend. She stood beside Toddles, petting and reassuring her pet, while the boyfriend hung back in the corner. Not the most well-kempt young man, he had what appeared to be dreadlocks and a poor attempt at a beard. He wasn't the kind of kid you'd want to see coming to pick up your daughter. The girl seemed to be genuinely concerned about Toddles. She was pretty, but she was dressed in black and had dyed black hair. Christie informed me later that this was called the "Goth" look. Toddles was really her mother's dog, but she was at work and had asked the young couple to bring her in. Other than their appearance, there was something else just not quite right about the pair. They seemed to be hiding something. It was like they were proud of the fact they knew something we did not.

"Has Toodles had any injuries lately that might have caused her nose to bleed?"

"No," the girl replied with a snicker.

"Do you think she could have gotten into any poisons or toxins?"

"I don't think so, but she does spend a lot of time under the porch, and I think my mom put some rat poison under there."

Christie stepped out to call the mother to confirm this, and I went on to examine the dog. Toddles didn't think that I needed to look in her mouth. She snarled and flashed her teeth at me, so I motioned for the boyfriend to give me a hand restraining her. He didn't seem overly happy about it, but he obliged so as to not look bad in front of the girl. Just as he slipped his arm under Toddles's neck to hold her, a couple of drops of blood fell onto his forearm. He proceeded to collapse, as if someone had let all the air out of him, hitting the linoleum with a thud.

"Christie, I need some help in here!" The girl was fawning over him like he was near death. I wanted to tell her to get a new boyfriend, but I held back, as usual. Christie got him up, then led him into a chair in the waiting room. A glass of water later, he was well on his way to recovery. Christie took over holding Toddles after it looked like the young man was going to live.

Sure enough, there were small hemorrhages on Toddles's gums and the insides of her lips, typical of rat-poison consumption, which causes a bleeding disorder. Rat poison interferes with vitamin K, an essential factor in the clotting process, making vitamin K replacement the preferred treatment.

I pulled up a syringeful of it to get Toddles started and Christie put together enough tablets to keep her going for the next month. Christie held the poodle still while I gave her a shot in the rear leg.

"Toddles has to have one of these pills once a day every day for the next month. We also need to see her back here in five days for a recheck." The girl just stared blankly at me. "She has to have the pills, or you could lose her."

She nodded at me this time, but I still didn't feel like she realized the gravity of the situation, so I motioned for Christie to step outside with me.

"I think we had better call her mother to make sure she gets the directions. The daughter just doesn't seem to be processing what I am telling her."

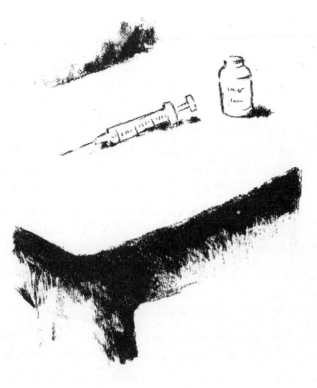

"She does seem a little out of it, and then there is the boyfriend."
She rolled her eyes and went off to call the mother.

Toddles managed to get her teenagers out the door, finally allowing us to get the next patient into the exam room for vaccinations. I
examined the easygoing cat and looked for the vaccine that Christie
usually set out for me on the counter, but it wasn't there.

"I'm sure I set that out before Toddles came in. I was trying to
keep things moving." She paused for a minute. "Well, maybe I just
thought that I did." Looking a little perplexed, she retrieved more
vaccine from the refrigerator in the back room.

We got the cat vaccinated and continued to see relatively uneventful cases for the rest of the afternoon. Once you get behind after working in a visit such as the one for Toddles, you are behind for the rest of the day. It makes for grumpy clients and often even grumpier patients. One particular cat was less than pleased that we didn't supply a separate waiting room for felines. She was extremely offended that she had to spend twenty minutes only a few feet from a dog. She carried the attitude with her right into the exam room, attempting to bite me when I tried to examine her ear.

Around six o'clock, the phone rang. Lorraine had already gone home, so Christie grabbed it. I could hear from her tone of voice as I listened through the open door of the exam room that it was something bad, but I tried to pretend it might not be. When she came through the door, interrupting my current appointment, I knew it was really not good.

"Dr. Wells, I think you'd better come to the phone."

Since Christie never addressed me this way, I knew something was up. I excused myself and walked out to the reception desk. Christie whispered in my ear, "You are not going to believe this one." She handed me the phone with way too big a smile on her face.

"Hello. This is Dr. Wells."

"Oh, Doctor, I want to thank you for taking such good care of Toddles today. You have no idea how much I appreciate it, but I have another problem now."

I braced myself for what was wrong with Toddles now. Whatever it was, it would surely be blamed on me, since I had just seen her.

"I just got home, and my daughter has informed me that she and that guy she calls her boyfriend gave themselves an injection while they were waiting for you to see Toddles." She began to cry. "I don't know what she has done to herself. These kids, what are they thinking? She was complaining of being tired, so I started to quiz her."

Where was the red phone, the direct line to the liability company, when you needed it? What in the heck could they have given themselves? I wondered. They could not have gotten anything too dangerous; those drugs were always locked up. I looked over at Christie and made a bewildered face.

She didn't speak, just mouthed the words *The vaccine!*

The missing vaccine, that was it! Right there on the exam room counter and in syringes in the cabinet underneath.

"Ma'am, I think your daughter and whatever you want to call him are going to be okay. Just call your doctor and ask him if he thinks feline distemper will be a problem. Have him call me if he has any questions. I can put him in touch with the manufacturer."

"Oh, thank you. I will let the boy's parents know, too. They are going to very upset with him, but relieved it was not something worse."

She thanked me again and hung up. It looked like no lawyers would be involved.

We finally saw the last patient about 7:30, but not before a client called in with a colicky horse. I would be going back out. I called Marion to let her know.

A candy bar and a Coke got me out and back. I walked in the house about 10:30. Marion and I discussed our days for a while, getting into bed a little after eleven o'clock. It was one of those days that I was just glad to see come to an end, even though I couldn't get the self-vaccinators out of my head. Hopefully, they wouldn't have any long-term effects from their little experiment.

Attorney Cat

"How much is this going to cost me?" demanded the well-dressed man in a pink golf shirt standing across the exam table from me.

On the exam table lay a beautiful gray cat curled up in a ball. She had a 104-degree temperature and an infection-filled lump the size of a Ping-Pong ball on the top of her head. These two findings alone were enough to explain her complete lack of interest in her surroundings. She had been in the clinic many times before for less traumatic reasons and was always full of life, but not now. The lump was an obvious abscess, most likely caused by the scratch or bite of another cat. Such wounds always got infected, but they were usually a relatively easy fix. A little drainage, combined with some oral antibiotics, should make her as good as new. The kitty's name was Madeline. The name had been given to her by Sarah, the little eight-year-old girl to whom she belonged. Sarah was the daughter of the attorney standing across from me, the one who was starting to get on my "Saturday-morning last nerve." Like most veterinary clinics, ours was open on Saturdays.

It was always the hardest day for me to work, since everyone else seemed to be out climbing mountains or enjoying some other Colorado activity. Now don't get me wrong: Some of my closest friends are attorneys. But of course "Mr. Attorney" had come in five minutes before closing without an appointment, even though Madeline had been sporting the bump for three days.

"You know, you just gave the cat her vaccinations two months ago. I wonder if the vaccine could have caused this," he said, interrupting my Saturday daze. I humored myself by imagining what it would take to give a conscious cat a shot in the middle of its head.

I finally responded. "I think it may be a little late for the vaccinations to have caused this." Having already explained the probable cause, I was becoming a little put off by his allegations.

Mr. Dimas had done very well at his law practice in Denver, but he hadn't made a lot of friends in the process. He just didn't know when to stop being an attorney outside the office. He was a little less than six feet tall, yet he had the knack of coming across as much larger than his actual size. His trick was to invade your personal space and speak just below a yell. That was what he was doing right then, leaning across the table, with his nose in my face.

"It will be about ninety-five dollars with the anesthesia and the antibiotics," I informed him.

"What if we skipped the anesthesia?" he replied with a sneer on his face. I ignored the comment. I'd found that doing so often had the most desirable effect.

"Madeline will be ready to be picked up in a couple of hours. I'll see you then?"

"Oh, no, I will be on the course by then." He seemed offended that I would think of interrupting his Saturday game.

Now I was really getting frustrated. "Okay, call me in the morning. I will try to meet you here."

Scooping up Madeline, I headed for the back room, but not quickly enough to dodge one last jab. "I suppose you are going to charge me for an overnight stay?"

Suppressing the urge to ask how much he charged an hour, I disappeared into the back. Christie was waiting for me in the treatment area. Her face was beet red from fighting back laughter. She knew that my aggravation was building, but her amusement with the situation brought me back down.

"I can't believe that guy beat you up so badly over the cost. Have you seen what he's driving?" She pointed to the parking lot, where he was getting into a huge gray Mercedes sedan. "I wonder how much that cost?" She giggled. Christie always got a kick out of what people drove, especially when they complained about money. She did have a valid point. The biggest complainers often drove the nicest cars.

With Madeline lying quietly on the stainless-steel treatment table,

Christie and I went to work on her. Christie drew up some short-acting anesthetic and I slipped it into the muscle in Madeline's leg. She barely flinched. The discomfort of the abscess outweighed the sting of the injection. Christie shaved the hair around the abscess, then scrubbed the area with thick brown Betadine soap. We had done this procedure so many times, we could practically do it with our eyes closed. Both of us donned latex gloves to protect ourselves, as you never knew what nasty bacteria lived in a cat abscess. In the Rocky Mountain region, they can even harbor the Black Plague, but that diagnosis usually includes swollen lymph nodes, which Madeline did not have. I made a small incision to drain the odiferous pus out, and then Christie flushed the deflated abscess with hydrogen peroxide. A penicillin injection and Madeline was finished. She would just have to room with us overnight so as not to interrupt golf. Just as Lorraine reached for the phone to turn it over to the answering service for the rest of the weekend, it rang.

"It's probably an emergency nail trim," Christie said with a sneer and an eye roll. "We are never going to get out of here today."

I gave my standard response just to be irritating. "Hot date?" That was always good for yet another eye roll, followed by a piercing glare. By this point, we had been working together too long.

Lorraine covered the mouthpiece on the phone. "She wants to talk to you. It's Madeline's little girl, Sarah." She handed the phone to me.

"Hi, this is Dr. Wells. May I help you?"

The little voice on the other end answered politely. "I am calling to check on my cat, Madeline. Is she going to be okay?"

"Oh, Madeline is going to be as good as new. She is all fixed up. She just needs to wake up from the anesthetic," I said, trying to assure her.

"Thank you so much for taking good care of her. She really is my best friend. I tell her everything." She paused for a second, then continued in a more pragmatic voice. "I also want to thank you for helping my dad. He can be a little hard to deal with sometimes. Mom says he is misunderstood, but he really is a good dad."

Quite a statement from an eight-year-old. She had been down this road before, apologizing for dear old dad. Even so, her sincerity made me feel as if I needed to give him another chance. I lied a little, acting as if dad had been on his best behavior in the clinic, and reassured her that Madeline would be fine.

"So it sounds like you and Mr. Attorney are best buds now," Christie said. She got way too much joy from listening in. It seemed to make staying late much more palatable for her.

Lorraine closed up the minute I got off the phone with Sarah. Christie gave me a "See ya" on her way out the back. I checked on little Madeline once more. She was starting to wake up from her induced sleep, wobbly and dazed. I reached into her cage and stroked her bobbing head.

"There's a little girl who misses you and can't wait to get you home. With dad's attitude, I think that you make a very good sounding board." Two hours later, I checked on her, and she was practically back to normal. I gave her some food, water, and another reassuring pat on the head for Sarah.

The next day was Sunday, and I stopped in to check on Madeline a couple of times, cleaning what was left of the abscess so she would look good when Sarah saw her. Having given up on Sarah's father, Marion and I decided to go out for pizza. As luck would have it, he paged me right after we'd ordered.

"I'm ready to pick up Madeline. I'll be over in just a few minutes."

"Well, we are out for dinner. How about an hour?" I replied.

"No way. My time is valuable and I have no other time to do it. I'm not waiting until tomorrow, either. You'll charge me for another day."

I thought of the little girl waiting at home and explained the situation to Marion. Now the pizza was to go—fine dining at the clinic. We ate our pizza in the back room as we waited, not the first or last time we shared pizza over the treatment table. Almost an hour later, the gray Mercedes lumbered up the driveway and a little girl jumped out on the passenger side. She came running in the front door ahead of her father. She had long dark hair and big brown eyes that glistened at the thought of getting her cat back.

"Where's Madeline?" she blurted. "Is she ready to go?"

I informed Sarah that Madeline was more than ready to go, then trotted off to the kennels to retrieve her. I encouraged Marion to wait in the back. I was afraid that her New York roots might kick in if Sarah's dad got confrontational. Northeasterners tend not to back down from a fight, which was not what we needed right then. She was cuddling Madeline in the back and handed her off to me.

No little girl was ever happier to have her kitty back, nor a kitty happier to see her little girl. Sarah held her tight to her chest, while Madeline purred with glee.

"Thank you, Doctor!" exclaimed Sarah. "Thank you so much. I can tell she feels better already."

"Well, how much is it?" her father asked, ruining the moment. Reluctantly, I handed him the bill, knowing it was not going to be received well. "All this for a cat. Well, I—"

"Dad," said Sarah, interrupting, "you promised Mom and me that you wouldn't act like this. Aren't you just glad that Madeline is feeling better?"

Dad grunted a few times in disgust, but even he couldn't deny a little girl who loved her cat. Without another word, he tossed his platinum card onto the counter. "Thanks again, Doctor, for both of us," Sarah yelled back as she walked out the door. I assumed she meant herself and Madeline.

A couple of days later, I heard Lorraine expounding at the front desk. "Oh my gosh, I can't believe this. Well, that little . . ." The expletives were followed by "Doc, you have to see this."

It was a letter from Sarah's father. It started with "I am writing to let you know I have contacted my credit card company and they will be denying the charges from your clinic." A bunch of legal jargon followed, but the bottom line was that a little leakage from Madeline's abscess (totally normal after such a procedure) had found its way onto his leather seats. He felt that what I'd charged for Madeline would be just enough to offset the cost of cleaning the seats. He went on to explain further that we were now even. The letter ended with "Thank you for your excellent service. I look forward to working with you next time Madeline has a medical issue."

I stood dumbfounded, while Christie laughed wholeheartedly. "Never trust an attorney in a Mercedes," she got in between snorts. "I don't think he sees anything wrong with it."

All I wanted to do was call him and tell him never to come back in to see me again, and that all further services would be denied from this point on. But I imagined little Sarah and how much she loved her kitty. That image kept me from reacting in anger.

By the following week, I had started to let go of the incident, although I had heartily enjoyed many attorney jokes in the meantime, oblivious to whom they may have offended. On Friday, Lorraine handed me a little pink envelope addressed to me. The card was from Sarah. "Thank you so much, Dr. Wells and Christie, for helping Madeline. P.S. Don't tell Dad, please!" Inside of the card was a folded check for the entire amount of Madeline's bill. It was from the personal account of Sarah's mother.

My frustration melted away and I remembered why I'd gone into veterinary medicine in the first place. It was to help animals, and if you can make a little girl happy along the way, then that is an extra bonus, even if her dad is a pain.

Surprise

It was a beautiful spring Sunday afternoon when the call came in that a three-year-old mare was not doing well. She had been developing a potbelly over the last couple of months, for which they had been deworming her frequently. In several species, a potbelly can be an indicator of an intestinal parasite or worms. But the last two days, the young mare had added "Off feed" to her list of symptoms, pushing the owners into calling me to take a look. Normally, a Sunday emergency would have irritated me just a little. They could have called me during the week, when the mare first started to look abnormal, but these people were otherwise the ideal clients. Besides being just plain good clients over the years, they had a sense of humor, were always grateful, and paid their bills on time. What more could one ask for?

They were about the same age as I was and I had grown to consider them friends over time. This relationship made the drive more palatable. I noticed the light green budding aspen and the wild iris along the way. Everything smelled clean and new after a long winter followed by a late spring. I rolled down my window to draw it all in, even sticking my arm out the window to let my palm bounce in the wind currents. I love all the seasons in the Rocky Mountains, but spring is most likely to bring out the child in all of the mountain dwellers. Even the elder deer in the herd that I passed played like fawns now that the snows had receded.

On my arrival, Amanda was waiting outside the barn door, pacing back and forth the width of the doorway. Like most pet owners, she was in that mind-set that the minute I showed up, everything would somehow be miraculously fine, no matter what the ailment. I think that in a pet owner's subconscious, he or she is no longer responsible for the problem upon the doctor's arrival and the veterinarian's presence relieves the person as the primary caregiver for the pet. Amanda did seem to relax when I got out of the truck and headed for the barn. At least the pacing subsided.

"I'm so glad you are here. Thanks for coming. I know that you hurried, but I thought you would never get here." She managed to conjure a smile.

The reason it had taken so long was that the area she lived in was very remote. There were about twenty houses in the same development, each with about ten acres, making it convenient to have horses. The homes and the land were very picturesque. To top it off, the whole enclave was surrounded by national forest, but it was in the middle of nowhere. From our house, it was almost an hour's drive over a couple of mountain passes and at least one river.

Amanda was an attractive small-framed woman who took great care of her horses. Up until recently, she'd had three horses, but ten months ago she and her husband had adopted a wild horse that had been brought in from the western slopes of Colorado. She was a lovely black three-year-old that had been rounded up for adoption when the herd had grown too large for the food supply in the area. They had picked her up at one of the prisons in Colorado where the inmates work with the wild horses so that their new owners can safely handle them. Because of the mare's background, they named her Wild Rose. Amanda and her husband had enjoyed Rose immensely over the last several months. She had really become a part of the family and was beginning to trust them. Now Amanda was afraid that they might lose her to whatever horrible illness she was afflicted with.

Following Amanda into the barn, which, by the way, was cleaner than most people's houses, I peered into the stall where the stricken animal stood. Yes, she had the symptoms that had been described—a potbelly, ribs showing a little more than normal on her sides, and a lack of enthusiasm about the fresh green hay that lay in front of her. I started to smile while rubbing my hand over the newly forming bald spot on the top of my head. Before I could get out my diagnosis, Amanda noticed my smile and was offended that I seemed to be finding humor in her mare's illness.

"What is so entertaining?" She was practically yelling. "I am about to lose my mare, and you think it's funny! What kind of veterinarian are you?"

I would have felt terrible if I really had not taken a distraught animal seriously, but this was not the case. I turned to the small woman staring at me red-faced and fuming.

"Amanda, your herd is about to grow from four to five," I proudly proclaimed. "When you adopted Rose, you got a two-for-one deal."

Now she was completely confused. I realized I would have to be a little more direct, so I tried again. "Rose is not sick. She is going to have a baby!"

Then a smile began to creep across her face. "Really, do you think so?"

"Yes, I'm pretty sure. We'll have to do a rectal palpation to be positive, but she has all the signs."

Now the red was gone and she was literally jumping up and down with relief. She even gave me a big hug.

I returned to the truck to grab a palpation glove and some sedative.

Normally, I wouldn't have needed to sedate a mare to check for pregnancy, but Rose had been completely wild until recently, and I was not willing to risk getting pummeled if she decided what I was about to do was completely unacceptable. Amanda was able to slip the halter over her head, then held her quietly while I slipped the needle into the jugular vein in her neck. Rose wasn't happy about the injection, swinging her head to flash me a glance, her ears pinned firmly back against her head.

I pushed in the tranquilizer while quietly trying to convince her it wasn't the end of the world. "Easy, girl, you will be much happier in a couple minutes."

Slowly, her head dropped and she had to concentrate more on standing than on what I was about to do. Amanda rubbed the mare's neck and talked softly to her while I proceeded to back up my diagnosis. After a quick palpation, I was able to announce with complete confidence that Rose was going to be a mother. Evidently, she must have gotten pregnant right before Amanda had adopted her. Since horses carry their babies for approximately eleven months, the timing would have been perfect.

Then came the question I always dreaded and tried to avoid. "When will the baby be born?" Amanda asked with great anticipation.

It is almost impossible for any veterinarian to answer this question exactly. There are just too many factors and variables. Like all mothers, mares don't all give birth on the exact day they are supposed to. Some wait a bit longer and some deliver sooner. But horse owners always want to know the precise minute when the foal will show up. They want to have the stall prepared, the video camera ready, and, in a perfect world, they would have their veterinarian waiting in the barn on standby. In reality, mares typically wait until no one is around. Just when the humans let down their guard and go inside to use the bathroom, the mare will make it happen.

The best answer is a noncommittal one. This time, I said, "Sometime in the next couple weeks."

I could tell that Amanda was not totally happy with the nonspecificity of my answer.

"Could you give me a little more specific guess?" she asked. Her use of the word *guess* indicated she was onto me. "You know that I will be sleeping in the barn until the baby comes, so the more accurate you can be would be helpful." She added, "My husband will not be happy with you if this goes on for two weeks!"

I had to hold my ground. Having been down this road before, I knew that pinning myself down on an exact birth date would do nothing but get me in trouble. It would mean phone calls in the middle of the night if the foal was not being born when I had said that it would be. So I stuck to my guns. "Sometime in the next two weeks."

Amanda shrugged and headed inside to get her sleeping bag. There is some deep-seated issue within horsewomen. They feel if they are not right there for the birth, the foal will not come, even though mares have been having foals on their own for thousands of years. You cannot convince them that they don't need to sleep in the barn, and if you did, it would be one of those rare instances when there was a birthing problem. I would rather deal with an angry husband sleeping alone than the scorn of a women whose horse was in distress at foaling. I got back in the truck, knowing that I would be back sometime in the next two weeks.

When the phone rang the next morning at daybreak, I was surprised to hear Amanda's voice. "Mia is here. You must come out right away."

In my morning daze, I wondered who the heck Mia was and why I needed to know that she was visiting. As I got my faculties together, Amanda explained that she had named the new foal Mia because it was May 1, and that she was waiting for me to examine her. I pulled on my clothing from the day before and told Marion where I was headed.

She was only able to mumble a "Have fun," then proceeded to roll over, wriggling back into the sheets.

I had kind of hoped she would go with me at this early hour, but I understood that more sleep sounded really good. After a Coke and doughnut at the local convenience store, I had enough caffeine and sugar in my bloodstream to drive the distance to Amanda's.

There she was again in front of the barn, pacing. "Everything okay?" I asked skeptically. I thought maybe something had gone wrong since we had talked.

"I just thought you would be here sooner," she said with furrowed brow as she spotted the empty Coke can on the dash and the frosting in my beard.

My junk-food stop had slowed me down too much and could have waited. Inside the barn, that familiar gentle sound of a mare talking to her newborn assured me that everything was fine.

"You said the foal would be born in the next two weeks. I never guessed it would be right away," Amanda chirped.

I wanted to act like I'd known it all along, but she never would have bought it. Though she did say that she had awakened her husband earlier to meet Mia and that he was elated the ordeal hadn't lasted two weeks. After his brief introduction to Mia, he'd gone back to bed.

I examined Mia, and she couldn't have been more normal. Amanda looked over my shoulder the whole time to make sure I didn't miss anything. I checked her over from head to tail, listening to her heart and lungs carefully to make sure there weren't any abnormalities. The baby's fine soft hair was curly from her mother's licking it dry, and she trembled slightly as I touched her with the stethoscope. This was her way of telling me it was a little cold. Lastly, I preformed the most undignified act of the exam on a new foal. The most common reason that foals don't nurse after they come into the world is constipation. Thus a preventative enema is usually advisable. Amanda held Mia's head while I administered the soapy liquid. As expected, the young horse felt that it was an unacceptable violation, especially so early in life. She bounced on her back legs, then popped me in the shins with both of her sharp little rear hooves. Fortunately, Mia was small enough that it didn't really do any damage, but the hit stung enough to bend me over.

Amanda snickered a little. "I'm sorry, I don't mean to laugh, but she has quite an attitude for a youngster."

"Yes, she is a real pistol," I agreed, "yet I can't really blame her." That pretty much defined Mia's and my relationship for the next several years. Mia never forgave me for that original indiscretion, after which even a simple vaccination became a life-threatening event for me. At one point, she even pinned me up against the wall just for trying to deworm her with some oral paste. I guess I couldn't really blame her for holding a grudge.

For Amanda, that first day of May was one to remember. She had the gift of a surprise baby instead of a dying mare. She was still a little miffed that I had not been more exact in my birth-time prediction, but she was glad that everything had ended well.

Waving to Amanda as I pulled out the drive, I yelled, "Call if there're any problems." She nodded her head and I sped off.

I was still a little dazed from getting up so early, since I'd planned on sleeping in just a little longer. Bottom line: I needed more caffeine. The nearest source was a wonderful little store not far from Amanda's place. The old stone building had been there since 1880 and had been run as a general store ever since its inception. Better yet, the lady who ran it was a direct descendant of the family that had started the store. Kathy, this generation's storekeeper, was in the back when I went in. Kathy quickly made her way to the front. I had been stopping here for many years and had never seen her with the knowing grin on her face that Kathy had now. She began ringing up my soda, and then she just couldn't take it anymore.

"So I hear Amanda's foal is doing fine despite your missing her birth date by so much," she said, still smiling.

I knew my mountain-practice world was small, but this was ridiculous. I started to explain, then realized it was futile. How many of my clients had already heard this story, and how skewed would it be? By that night, I was sure that the rumor would be that I had missed the date by at least two months.

Fortunately, these situations don't bother me so much these days. The fact that both mare and foal were fine was what was really important. Besides, that's why they call it the "practice" of veterinary medicine.

Won't Bite

H e's never tried to bite anybody in his whole life." This is one of every veterinarian's favorite quotes. It is one of those comments that makes the experienced veterinarian sit up and take notice, especially on a Saturday afternoon when the rest of the staff has gone home. It's the type of comment that turns on that lightbulb somewhere in the back of one's brain. In real-life veterinary practice, the phrase translates to "This dog is going to try to bite me."

Even though the client may be telling the truth and his pet is the sweetest animal on the planet, no one may have done anything to it before that was painful. It's been loved, played with, maybe even wrestled with, but nobody has ever attempted to give it an injection or treat its laceration.

Veterinary students are not warned about this "never bites" syndrome. I'm not sure if that's because the professors have never heard it or if they chuckle to themselves, knowing their students will eventually find out on their own. I definitely didn't see it mentioned in any textbooks. It should absolutely have been the first thing on the first page of *Introduction to Canine Medicine* in very bold letters: "If a client tells you that his dog never bites . . ."

Fortunately, I was imparted this wisdom before a pooch ever sunk its choppers into my flesh. I attended a local veterinary continuing-education program within the first couple of months after graduation. The meeting was held in the back room of a steak house, unchanged since the sixties. It was complete with imitation-wood paneling and neon Budweiser signs with Clydesdale horse figurines. The whole place was so infiltrated with decades of cigarette smoke that even the food was tainted. Ten of us sat around a rectangular table and listened to a relatively short talk about flea treatment from a pharmaceutical company's representative. Like most of these types of get-togethers, some of the best information is dispensed during the postspeech conversations, when everyone kicks back in their chairs and the facade slips away. It is then that practitioners will give up the less than glamorous details of what has happened to them over the years, stories they might not have expounded upon in the sterile atmosphere of their clinics.

Dr. Wood was the eldest member of the group. No one particular person was the designated leader of the group, but it was just understood that if leadership was required, he was the one. He had a head of wavy gray hair, along with more hard-earned wrinkles on his face than anyone else in the group. His laugh was loud and infectious, but when he was serious, his eyes would squint, staring right through new grads like me.

That night, the postpresentation conversation was mostly loud and jovial. The doctors told the usual old tales of antics from veterinary school, the kind that got more extravagant every time they were told. There was laughter and backslapping, until one of the younger doctors rolled back his sleeve to expose his forearm. It was severely bruised, discolored, and riddled with punctures.

"I had a big dog get hold of my arm this week. I didn't think I was ever going to get him off."

Everyone in the crowd ground to near silence as they stared at the painful-looking swollen arm on display in front of them.

"It was a huge mixed-breed dog. I'm not sure what he had in him. He didn't even growl. I was just checking his hips, and the next thing I knew, he had me."

After the shock of the wound's appearance wore off, everyone in the crowd picked up again and began comparing dog-bite scars as if they were war wounds.

"Got this one in '82," one veterinarian said, pointing with pride to a two-inch scar on the top of her hand.

Another one lifted his shirt to expose a row of punctures on his side in the distinct pattern of a dog's incisors. The third didn't have to raise his shirt or pull up a sleeve to reveal his scar. It was just to the right side of his nose. There was still a divot nearly half an inch deep and three-quarters of an inch in diameter. We all knew it was there, but no one really noticed it anymore. He just pointed to it with his index finger.

"Canine tooth of a chow. I never even saw it coming. I'm lucky she didn't get my eye." He raised his glass of wine to the rest of the group.

That was when Dr. Wood leaned over and whispered in my ear, "If they say they never bite . . ." Evidently, someone had forgotten to tell him this early on, since his hands were covered with scars.

"I always tell the young veterinarians before they find out the hard way. Some vets never recover from that first bad bite. They're just never the same after the big one."

I had to admit he was right about that. I had a friend in veterinary school who, after a devastating bite from a very scared German shepherd, never treated a dog again and now only works on cows.

I heeded the words of the infamous Dr. Wood, being overly cautious whenever I heard the words *won't bite* uttered.

When I heard the Ryans say similar words that Saturday at the clinic, I didn't put myself on guard as much as usual, possibly because they were more than a little inebriated, making me frustrated early on. They were a very nice couple who just really liked to have a good time. Mr. Ryan was a large man, about fifty-five, with his long graying brown hair stuffed into a ponytail. He was half leftover hippie and half aging biker. His wife was only thirty-five, though she looked a little older.

They both held their dog Mick's head while I examined the cut over his right hip. It was not severe, but it would require a few sutures. He'd gotten in a fight with a neighbor's dog and had come home sporting this little trophy.

"You should see the other dog," Mr. Ryan boasted.

I didn't acknowledge his testosterone-fueled comment. I'd treated too many dog-fight wounds after hours and had heard it all before. I wanted to remind him that we had a leash law in our county and that he would be fined if the sheriff found out. But I knew it was useless to bring this up with a man as under the influence as he was.

"I'm going to need to anesthetize Mick to suture up his laceration. Do you think you can hold him while I give him an IV injection?"

"Oh yeah! We can do it. No problem, Doc. Besides, he never—"

"I know, never bites."

To make matters worse, Mick was a large male rottweiler, unneutered, of course. He probably weighed 120 pounds, all of it muscle, which was more than I could say for Mr. Ryan.

I drew up the anesthetic, holding Mick's leg with my left hand while fishing for his vein with my right. As I slipped the sharp bevel of the needle under Mick's thick skin, I was concentrating too much on my goal to see Mick shake loose from the alcohol-weakened grip of the Ryans and swing his head down in the direction of my hand. By the time his black nose came into my field of vision and the leg began to pull away from my needle, it was too late. It was another one of those times when the motion-picture frame of life grinds down to slow motion and you feel as if you are watching the action from a theater seat rather than directly in front of you. I jerked my hand away and watched in astonishment as it cleared Mick's jaws as they came together—that is, almost cleared them. Mick's canines caught the end of my index finger just before it made it out of his mouth. The sharp end of the top tooth connected with my fingernail and the bottom one with the fleshy fingertip underneath. My finger was already on the way out, so it slipped out of the grasp before a gaping wound could be created, resulting in more of a "pinching" wound. The syringe bounced on the floor.

"Oh . . . crap." I resisted the urge to use more descriptive words in front of even these clients.

The Ryans giggled a little under their alcohol-laden breath. "We're sorry, we didn't mean to let him go."

I wanted to respond, Yeah, it was real hard for him to get away from you two. But I just gripped my now-throbbing finger, throwing them a sharp glance.

The "pinch" didn't seem to hurt, but a blood blister was beginning to develop under the fingernail, resulting in an astronomical increase in pain. My pain level was directly disproportionate to my patience level with the buzzed Ryans. I knew I had to get them out of the clinic before the situation deteriorated, but Mick still had to be sedated.

I figured I could give him an injection in the muscle of the unin-jured rear leg if the Ryans could hold him and I could manage the syringe with my left hand. At least if I was able to give an injection in the rear end, I might have time to get out of the way if his head swung around.

"Do you think that you two could hold him this time if I tried to give him a shot in the butt?"

"Oh sure, we can do it. We won't let him go this time, Doc." I think that my postbite demeanor sobered them up a little.

Pulling up a new syringeful of sedative, I held my breath. They both grasped Mick around the neck again, almost lying on him to keep him still. Mick wiggled and growled a little, inducing more snickers from the happy couple. I was just able to get the needle in and the syringe plunger down before Mick broke loose again.

"Okay. Let's put him in a kennel until he goes to sleep; then I can patch him up.

The Ryans, looking like they were the ones who had received the injection, carried Mick to a kennel in the back room. I wasn't much help, as I had only one usable hand at this point.

"Now you guys can go home and I'll take care of him."

Often clients would have fought me on this, wanting to stay to help, but fortunately that was not the case with the Ryans.

Mrs. Ryan spoke up right away. "Great, we can go to the bar."

"Now honey, remember the last time we were there you got kicked out for dancing on the table. You can't do that again," Mr. Ryan re-sponded.

His wife acknowledged that she would not repeat her past perfor-mance, and then the couple stumbled out the door. Luckily, the bar they were headed for was only a short distance away.

After they were gone, I was able to writhe in pain by myself.

The blister had grown under my fingernail, making the pressure almost too much to take. I wrapped my damaged appendage to protect it, then checked in on Mick to see if the sedation had kicked in yet.

He was snoring blissfully in the kennel. I had given him just a tinge more than the recommended dosage, not wanting to risk another attack. Knowing it wasn't his fault, I patted him on the head. "I know, big fellow. It hurts, and I would be a little defensive, too. Not to mention that I'm sure you have parent issues on top of it."

The Ryans had taken good care of him, even bringing him in to have his wound dealt with when they were toasted. Yet, there was a certain attitude that had rubbed off on Mick from the Ryans—a kind of macho guard-dog mentality. I didn't even want to know what they may have needed him to guard.

Even though I felt sorry for Mick because of what had been bestowed on him, I still wasn't taking any chances. I placed a light gauze wrap around his mouth, just in case he suddenly arose from his stupor while I was working. He was much too heavy for me to lift him up on the treatment table in my disabled state, and I really didn't want to call Christie in after hours, so I sutured up his laceration right there in the kennel. The real trick was doing it one-handed.

Just after I finished with Mick, the phone rang. I grabbed it before the call was forwarded to the answering service, clearing my throat to answer.

"Hey, Doc, how's Mick doing?" Mrs. Ryan asked in a voice even more slurred than it had been an hour and a half before.

"Oh, he's fine. He'll be ready to go home in the morning."

After a little hesitation, she said, "We'll probably get there a little closer to noon, but give him a kiss for me."

That wasn't going to happen. I had to draw the line somewhere when it came to client requests. He got a pat on the head instead.

Mick woke up with no problems, as good as new. He even seemed appreciative, giving me a few licks on the hand. I wrote out specific instructions concerning follow-up care and when to remove the sutures. I had a couple of large-animal calls to make on Sunday, so Christie agreed to meet them at noon to discharge Mick.

Monday morning, she met me at the door with a smile on her face. "So, do you want to tell me about your Saturday with the Ryans?"

I looked a little bewildered, so she produced a package from behind the reception counter. "The Ryans left this for you."

It was a bottle of spirits with a small piece of notepaper attached. On it the Ryans had scribbled, "Thanks for everything, Doc."

Unicorn

The January wind stung my face and hands to the point of painful numbness, exacerbating the arthritis that years of practice had induced in my thumbs. Bone-chilling air crested the Continental Divide and raced down into the valley, where I stood. It was like being in a snow globe while someone was shaking it sideways.

"Why don't you wear your gloves to do that, Doc?" is a question that I had been asked many times and that had always irritated me just a bit.

I know that it appeared kind of stupid not to wear gloves, but those who asked had never attempted to manipulate small metal instruments in tight spaces, let alone while wearing bulky gloves. It was hard enough to get my bare fingers into the handles of the hemostats, and bulky gloves were not going to help. Sometimes on days like this, I would wear plastic surgery gloves to cut the wind and keep my hands dry, but they would always tear early on in this extreme cold and become useless.

The reason for my discomfort this day was the fact that I was standing outside in the wind, removing small splinters of wood from the frontal sinuses of a horse. Lance was a beautiful bay with a star on his forehead, but half an hour before, he had looked more like a unicorn than a horse, complete with the mythical horn. He had been found that morning with a foot-long, two-inch-thick stick protruding out of his head, right between his eyes. I have to admit the spectacle even threw me off a little when I first pulled into the McClures' driveway.

"He got out of his pen last night about nine and ran off into the timber. I think a mountain lion scared him." Mr. McClure looked a little terrorized himself when he talked about it.

There had been a lot of mountain lion sightings in that area during the last month. In fact, another client of mine, just a couple miles away, had had an older horse killed by one just a week before.

He continued: "He showed up this morning looking like this. Do you think there is anything that you can do?"

One of the amazing things about horses is that they can have horrid-looking injuries, but as long as nothing vital is damaged, they will most likely survive. While running through a lodgepole-pine forest in the middle of the night until you ram a stick into your forehead is a bad idea, this horse would probably be fine.

After giving him some sedative, I had managed to wiggle the wooden horn out of his sinuses and was now picking out the pieces that were left behind. The wound was approximately two inches wide and an inch and a half deep, but the stick had missed his eyes, not going deep enough to damage his brain. The sinus cavities of the horse not only serve their expected functions but also act as a shield to protect the important stuff in the head—sort of a first line of defense for animals that tend to look for a way to hurt themselves.

"I just can't believe he is going to be okay, Doc."

Mr. McClure was a medium-size man in his mid-thirties. He had thick red hair, with just the hint of gray beginning to show at the temples. Always an agreeable man, he now was just elated that his stepson's horse was going to make it without permanent damage. Mrs. McClure had a son from a previous marriage. This son, Jay, had been born with some birth defects, for which he'd had multiple surgeries during his first six years of life. Jay's father had not been able to handle it and had left Jay and his mom to deal on their own. The procedures had left some physical scars and had inhibited Jay's growth, but he was an amazing kid and smart as a whip.

When Mr. McClure first married Jay's mother, he had purchased an older pony for Jay. Jay was about seven at the time and small for his age, so the pony was perfect for him. The pony took great care of the boy. He was able to learn to ride without getting hurt. The experience gave him mental confidence while also helping his muscles and balance to develop.

The problem with great old ponies is that they cannot live forever. In the fall of the previous year, the pony had been losing weight, so the McClures called me out to take a look. His teeth were in bad shape, and when I attempted some dental work, three of the ancient teeth just fell out onto the ground. To make it worse, Jay was watching the whole thing, tearing up at the sight of his pony's teeth in the dirt.

"What have you done to him?" he choked out between tears.

I tried to explain how horse's teeth continually wear off, so when they get down to nothing, they simply fall out. But he never really bought it.

The pony continued to go downhill, and three weeks later I had to put the poor thing down. This does not make you a hero in a child's mind, so getting Lance back to as perfect as possible today was very important to me, as well. It was a chance to redeem myself in Jay's eyes.

Mr. McClure had purchased the new horse for Jay as a Christmas surprise, after having me check him over. Lance passed the prepurchase exam with flying colors. He was the perfect age for Jay, just under twelve. Plenty of experience, but young enough to have a long life with Jay. I even worked on his teeth without any coming out and gave him all his vaccinations on Christmas Eve, so he was all ready to go for Christmas morning.

Jay fell in love with him immediately, naming him Lance, after his favorite knight of the Round Table. Now, only a month later, the "knight" had managed to nearly kill himself with a wooden spear to the head. In order to shield Jay from what the McClures thought might be a life-threatening injury, they had hustled him off to school before he could see Lance with his extra appendage.

"We couldn't bear to have him see Lance this way after so recently losing his pony." Mr. McClure seemed to choke up just a bit when he brought this up. He really cared a lot about his stepson and didn't want him to get hurt. "He's been through so much in his short life, and he loves this horse so much."

It was one of those times when the pressure to make the patient better was almost too much. Too many times in my career I'd had kids look up at me for the answers with tears in their eyes and I'd had to tell them that their beloved pet wouldn't make it. Fortunately, today was not going to be one of those times. Lance looked bad, but he was going to be fine.

After I removed the last tiny piece of branch I could find from his head wound, I found enough skin to suture across the hole to nearly draw it closed. The head of any animal is the most forgiving when it comes to healing. From experience, I knew that this wound would heal, leaves just a small scar and an indentation, as long as we could keep it from getting infected.

After giving Lance an injection of antibiotic and some anti-inflammatory to keep the swelling on his head to a minimum, I made a special effort to clean all the blood off his face. I attempted to make the wound as acceptable as possible for Jay when he got home.

Handing Mr. McClure a white plastic container of antibiotic powder, I said, "Two scoops once a day in his feed, and I'll be back to check him on Saturday."

"Great! Jay will be here then, and I'm sure he'll have a few questions for you." He smiled.

I waved good-bye and headed back to the clinic. I felt as if I was

cheating a little, but by Saturday I would have a better idea how Lance's wound was doing, so the questions would be easier to answer.

I didn't hear from the McClures over the next two days, which I considered to be a sign that things were going fairly well. The weather on this day was completely different from what it had been the first day I treated Lance. There wasn't a cloud in the sky, and the bright sun lit up the snow-frosted mountains as far as one could see in any direction. Pulling up to the house, I saw the little outline of Jay holding Lance's lead rope and feeding him carrots as he awaited my arrival. The horse would wiggle his soft lips, gently slipping each carrot from Jay's hand as it was offered. Jay would, in turn, give Lance a big hug around the neck after each carrot.

"How are we doing today?" I said loudly as I walked up to the two, hoping not to jolt either one of them.

They both turned to look, and I could now see the wound on Lance's head. It actually looked pretty good. Several drops of reddish fluid had oozed out and were now frozen in the hair just above his nose, but some drainage was to be expected.

"How do you like the way it looks today, Dr. Wells?" Jay asked with caution in his voice. "He's going to be okay, isn't he?"

"It looks good and he is going to be fine," I said as I began to clean up Lance's face.

"How many stitches did you have to put in?" This was the typical question that all kids asked when you had sutured up a wound on their pet. The number of stitches indicated the severity of the injury, and they also liked to have a number to tell their friends.

"Only a few. The wound was not that big; it was just deep."

"Do you think it will leave a scar?" Although this was also a typical question, it held much more meaning coming from this particular little boy.

I looked down at Jay's face, which was marked by the scars of surgeries to correct his birth defects. He looked back at me with complete sincerity in his eyes. He really wanted to know if Lance's wound would leave a permanent mark.

"It will probably leave a small scar after it heals, but I don't think that it will affect him in any way."

He continued to look at me for a moment, then appeared to accept my answer and move on. He told me how many sutures he'd had during his reconstructive surgeries, pointing out the scars that went with each. All I could think of was how tough it must have been for such a young boy to have gone through so much. Then for his father to take off was almost too much to bear. This was a boy who really needed someone to talk to who would always listen, never judging, and Lance was that someone.

Jay kept asking me questions about equine wounds while I cleaned up Lance's face and flushed his head wound with an iodine solution. Jay resumed feeding Lance carrots to keep his mind off my treatment.

"I know that it hurts, so I want to make it as easy on him as possible. I know the carrots distract him from the pain," Jay said matter-of-factly.

I finished by packing as much antibiotic ointment into the open part of the wound as possible. I gave the sweet horse a quick pat on the chest, then knelt down in front of the perceptive little boy. There was so much wisdom and compassion in those young eyes.

"Jay, what do you want to be when you grow up?" I asked.

"Well, I really thought I wanted to be a veterinarian for horses, but I know I won't be strong enough to do that. So I want to be either a research veterinarian or a doctor for children like me."

I usually don't have to fight back tears very often, but now I felt my eyes begin to sting. Standing up quickly, I rubbed Jay's head, fluffing up his hair.

"I know that you can do whatever you want. Don't let anyone tell you otherwise."

"Oh, I know," he replied, giving Lance a big hug. "My parents tell me the same thing."

I told Jay to let his stepfather know that I would be back in exactly one week to remove Lance's sutures. Jay promised me that he would be there, too, and waved vigorously as I pulled out of the driveway.

The following Saturday, I went back and found Jay and Mr. Mc-Clure standing in front of the house with Lance. Jay was feeding him apples now and was working his way through a fairly large bag of them. Lance seemed to be putting on more than a few pounds during his recovery, so a chat about obesity in horses might have to be in all of their futures. The term *kill them with kindness* was a reality here.

"The wound is healing great, Doc," Mr. McClure yelled as I walked toward them. "Jay has been tending to it every day, keeping the area real clean. Hasn't he been doing a great job?"

"It does look very good. I think we'll be able to take the sutures out today."

Jay looked up at me, beaming from ear to ear.

"Jay, ask Dr. Wells the question you had for him."

Jay hesitated for a moment, then cautiously asked, "Do you think that I could take out the sutures?"

Now I hesitated. It would be great to let Jay do this. He could tell this story for weeks at school, but my liability company would not be at all pleased. I could just imagine explaining this one in court. "So, Dr. Wells, you picked up a small boy, who had already been through many reconstructive surgeries, and let him remove the sutures from the head of a thousand-pound horse? What were you thinking?"

But I remembered the first time the local veterinarian had let me really do something. So I gave Lance a small dose of sedative first.

I dug my suture-removal scissors out of the truck. They had a little hook on the end to make it easy to pull the suture away from the skin before snipping it. This gadget made it easier for a first-timer.

Lance's head dropped down from the sedation, so I didn't have to lift Jay very far. He was even lighter than I'd expected. His bone density and muscle tone just was not as developed as those of a typical nine-year-old boy, so it was not a burden at all for me to hold him as he worked to remove each suture.

Lance cooperated more than just a horse who'd had a little tranquilizer. He was keeping as still as possible for his favorite boy.

I put Jay back down and Lance raised his head back up.

"Thanks, Dr. Wells. That was great!" Jay exclaimed. "Wait until I tell my friends."

"Wait. I didn't get a picture!" Mr. McClure ran back into the house and then reappeared with his camera.

I held Jay up again to pose, and with a little coaxing, Lance graciously dropped his head for the photo shoot. Mr. McClure thanked me several times as he followed me back to the truck.

"You have no idea how much Jay and I appreciate everything. You know, I really didn't totally believe you that morning when you pulled that stick out of Lance's head. I didn't believe he would heal this well."

A week later, I received a thank-you note from Jay with a copy of the picture his father had taken of his first medical procedure. He wrote that after Lance's injury, he had decided to go to medical school and become a plastic surgeon.

Today, Jay is halfway through his surgical residency.